Dying to Find My Laughing Place

A Search for Contentment

Dying to Find My Laughing Place

A Search for Contentment

By

Andrea Gehrett

This book is wholly dedicated to my Lord Jesus Christ.

Acknowledgements:

I want to thank my loving husband, Howie, for his endless support and for selflessly managing the household. You never complained about working in hot attics or being covered in itchy insulation and other undesirable things as I retreated to a mountainous paradise for solitude to concentrate on this project. I am lucky to have you! I also want to thank my momma for being my supreme travel companion and chief cook serving me day in and day out during my writing retreat. My deepest appreciation also goes to my daddy not only for his love and support, but also for generously sending us over the continental divide on the road less traveled giving us access to incomprehensible views which refreshed my tired writing brain. And to my children, thank you for patiently enduring countless hours of editing with me intently fixed on a manuscript. My family deserves my full attention, and I acknowledge the quality time sacrificed in this endeavor. I love you all and am blessed by your support.

I am grateful to Wayne for giving me paid time off to vacate my station and go write. I am also grateful for all my donors. Some gave above and beyond what they were already sacrificing to help offset costs. Further, I appreciate my prayer team who blessed me with faithful petitions asking for this work to be led by the Spirit.

Thank you to my peer reviewers, Richard and Paul, for jotting down many notes, giving me candid feedback, and enduring the roughest draft. Much appreciation also goes to Wendy for her time and mad skills in editing all subsequent drafts. My deepest gratitude is extended to Stacy for stepping forward and volunteering to do all the typesetting and self-publishing. And to Sonia, thank you for graciously working through many nit-picky graphic design revisions; I am touched by your patience and kindness. For all involved, I am blessed by the gifts each of you contributed to this book.

As this project was launched, the vision of The Power Plant was given, and a new ministry was birthed. Formation of the new ministry called for a logo. Thank you, Shane, for generously volunteering your time to design The Power Plant logo in conjunction with this project.

Finally, I want to acknowledge all the friends and colleagues over the years who have shared life moments with me and left an imprint. And for the people whom I savagely offended in years past and neglected to apologize when the opportunity existed, I acknowledge that an apology is way past due. This story is also for you... hope that lives can be changed and redeemed through the power of Christ.

Contents:

Introduction

Does God care? That was the question burning deep within my heart after struggling for nearly a decade. I recently turned forty and, even though my youthful appearance seems to be fleeting and I can now check the box as middle-aged, I feel relieved to have weathered the storms of my thirties. Those years were marked with some tough life lessons. Of course, not every day was bad in that season of my life. There were many good times and fond memories stored in the bank, but much of my thirties was spent grappling with deep questions.

I'd be willing to bet that everyone has wrestled with the same types of questions regardless of background or belief. Circumstances may differ, and the search for an answer may take differing lengths of time for different people. Whether the questions of our hearts are plainly stated or not, the core issues are that we long to make peace with how a loving God could allow

11

this, and why He wouldn't save us from *that* if He is truly a loving God and cares for us.

This book tells my story of discovering the true value of who I am and the purpose behind my pain. It is the journey of a woman desperately searching for lasting contentment in a world with many quick fixes and home remedies. Truthfully, I didn't want to write this book. I was wildly opposed to the idea each time it was presented to me, and for nearly five years I tabled any discussion about writing it. Publicly sharing would expose my inner self and make me vulnerable; it was easier to justify that I had nothing to offer.

But I do have something to offer. I have my experiences, failures, and lessons learned. I have embraced being vulnerable, because acknowledging these experiences means something to me now. I see the opportunity in taking full responsibility for how I felt, how I responded, and how I came to be the person I am today. Sharing these things can help someone else who is struggling. Perhaps that is you.

This narrative is not about retelling all the nitty-gritty details of hard times or even assigning blame to another person. It is about my journey. How I came to terms with who I am and what I believe. We all must do it, but to what extent do we spend the effort in knowing ourselves more fully? There is incomprehensible value in going through the discovery process.

What I believe may be different from what you believe. I am a Christian. The whole basis of Christianity is built on love and how that love is exemplified in the person of Jesus Christ, so it is not my place to condemn you if you don't believe what I believe. That would be contrary to the principles of my faith. It is my hope that if you do stand on a different belief that you would not consider my story as some stranger's calculated Bible-thumping persuasive platform, but rather see it as a true heart testament of a life changed by a passionate and loving God.

I became a Christian at age eleven, but I hadn't experienced much growth in my faith until later on when the storms of life began to brew. I struggled with the dysfunction that came into my life upon arrival of the rainy season and had no idea how to handle the overwhelming nature of raw emotion. The discovery of who I am revealed that I knew much about Christianity but very little about my own heart and spirit. I didn't know how to connect what I knew in my head to what I was feeling in my heart. Not knowing how to apply Christian principles left me feeling powerless, and I eventually came to understand that I lacked the spiritual depth needed to serve as my steady anchor in the middle of a storm. Unfortunately, before I recognized that truth, I had become one of the people that author Chip Dodd speaks about in his book *Voice of the Heart*, "We ended up as adults who don't know how to use our feelings in order to live fully. Consequently, we don't know how to handle our woundings except by being more defensive, survival oriented, or self-sufficient. We develop philosophies that excuse our own impairments, and we eventually become wounders ourselves."

Who really wants to be a wounder? I certainly didn't. What do you do when you have the sobering realization that the storm has taken you off the charted course and landed you on the island of no fun? As I sat shipwrecked and drenched with despair, I wondered how it would be possible to leave discontentment behind and never return to the forsaken island. Brainstorming for good ideas and relying on self-help theology led me nowhere. At this time, a story from my childhood began to permeate my thoughts and became a catalyst to kick off my quest for contentment.

This childhood favorite of mine is a tale taken from the work of Joel Chandler Harris in the late 1800s which Disney made into an animated movie in 1946. The movie was called *Song of the South*. The story is about an old sharecropper named Uncle Remus who befriends a brokenhearted little boy named Johnny. Uncle Remus had a sunny disposition and was a master storyteller, and he introduced Johnny to the tales of Brer Rabbit with the hopes that they would brighten Johnny's day. Brer Rabbit was the main character in all of his folk tales, and most of them involved him being chased by two opponents, Brer Fox and Brer Bear.

One of the tales Uncle Remus told Johnny was about the laughing place. You see, Brer Rabbit had been caught by Brer Fox and Brer Bear and taken to their den on Chickapin Hill. They had cinched him with rope from head to toe on a roasting skewer over an open flame, leaving nothing to dangle loosely except his big, floppy ears. They were going to roast him like a rotisserie chicken, so he had to think quickly how to get himself out of the mess.

All of a sudden, Brer Rabbit began to laugh hysterically. Confused, they asked why he was laughing. Brer Rabbit cunningly told them he had just been to his laughing place. Brer Fox, aware of Brer Rabbit's tricky schemes to get out of trouble, was a little wary when Brer Rabbit said he would show them his laughing place if only they'd untie him. Brer Bear was dying with curiosity to see this place, and even though Brer Fox wasn't so quick to fall for the scam, Brer Bear was the bigger of the two and won the argument to let Brer Rabbit off the skewer so they could see the mysterious laughing place.

Brer Rabbit took them into the woods and found a spot in the brush to point out as his laughing place. At his insisting, they moved in. Closer. Into the thicket until a hornet's nest fell snugly onto Brer Bear's head. The two were swarmed and stung while Brer Rabbit steadily backed away from them. Once Brer Bear popped the nest off his head and found his nose enlarged and bright red, he raged with anger and gruffly stated, "You said this was a laughin' place. And I ain't laughin'." Brer Bear was about as sharp as a marble, and Brer Rabbit knew that as he rolled further away in laughter and responded, "I didn't say it was *your* laughin' place. I said it was *my* laughin' place, Brer Bear." Once again, Brer Rabbit made a smooth escape.

As soon as Uncle Remus finished his tale, Johnny and his friend Ginny were wide-eyed with excitement and burst forth:

Johnny: I wish I had a laughin' place.

Ginny: Me, too.

Uncle Remus: What makes you think you ain't? 'Course you got a laughin' place.

Johnny: Really, Uncle Remus?

Ginny: Really?

Uncle Remus: Everybody's got one. The trouble is, most folks won't take time to go look for it.

Johnny/Ginny: Where's mine?

Uncle Remus: Well, now, that I can't exactly say. 'Cause where 'tis for one mightn't be where 'tis for another.

Johnny: Come on, Ginny. Let's start looking.

This is exactly how I began my search. I felt like a little kid sitting at the feet of Uncle Remus with Johnny and Ginny. I was dying to find my laughing place. My joy. My contentment. But so far I hadn't been able to find it. Not even a giggle.

The chapters in this book tell you what I've discovered in finding my laughing place. How many times have we heard the phrase, "I wish I knew now what I didn't know then"? Looking back, I wish I had been introduced long before my storms hit to the concepts taught by Arthur Pink in his discussion *A Fourfold Salvation from Sin*. In his work, he basically points out the process Christians go through in relation to sin. Once we make a decision to follow Christ and accept Him as our savior, we are freed from the penalty of sin, but all throughout our life we must grow to become more like Christ and learn to be free from the *power* of sin. One day we will spend eternity free from the presence of sin, but for now, while we live in this world, we must stare sin in the face each day and decide what to do with it. Will we let it rule us, or will we overcome it?

My sin contributed to my discontentment. No one can fight the battle of sin in their own strength — though I gave it my best shot for a very long time. As Christians, Jesus promised us the indwelling gift of the Holy Spirit to be our navigational beacon and the key to overcoming sin. I didn't fully realize I had abundant power to weather life's storms, and in my spiritual ignorance (and similar to the path taken by Brer Bear), I was dumb enough to go off searching for the physical place that made me happiest. It stung to learn that the more I tried to find happiness in my own strength, the more I found myself disappointed.

I could wish to have chosen more wisely in applying principles of my faith. It sure would have circumvented a lot of trouble if I had done so, but the truth is that I'm stubborn and I had to learn things the hard way. We grow through mistakes made, and the result of my storms brought me closer to God, producing an intimate relationship that has proven to never fail.

It has been discovered that my faith in Jesus is where my laughing place is. For me, true contentment goes no further than the cross of Christ, and there is nothing this world can offer that even comes close to comparing to the lasting satisfaction I've found with my heavenly Father.

God loves us so much that He longs to have a meaningful relationship with each of us, and just as any loving parent would discipline their child in order to teach what is best, our heavenly Father does the same. I was not, and still am not, exempt from this principle. There is no question in my mind that God cares. He does. Any lingering doubt in my mind has been abolished this side of my fiercest storms, and I believe Arthur Pink accurately summarizes in his sermon notes from long ago the "why" that is so applicable to my journey, and yours too:

> *God so orders His providences that our earthly nest is destroyed.*
> *The winds of adversity compel us to leave the downy bed of carnal*
> *ease and luxuriation. Grievous losses are experienced in some form*
> *or other. Trusted friends prove fickle, and in the hour of need fail us.*

The family circle, which had so long sheltered us and where peace and happiness was found, is broken up by the grim hand of death. Health fails and weary nights are our portion. These frying experiences, these bitter disappointments, are another of the means which our gracious God employs to save us from the pleasure and pollution of sin. By them He discovers to us the vanity and vexation of the creature. By them He weans us more completely from the world. By them He teaches us that the objects in which we sought refreshment are but 'broken cisterns,' and this that we may turn to Christ and draw from Him who is the Well of living water, the One who alone can supply true satisfaction of soul.

It is my prayer that this is a story which many of you can relate to, whether you consider yourself a Christian or not. Life is hard and struggles are real. Perhaps your struggles are different, but basic emotions felt with any challenge are the same. Maybe you haven't endured a divorce or grieved the loss of a child, but you have experienced sadness on some level, and it is in this way that you will be able to connect with what I write.

I hope that I am able to clarify that Christianity is not about pretending to be perfect or placing ourselves above anyone else. A wand is not magically waved at the moment of salvation, so that we instantaneously have life all figured out. To the contrary, being a follower of Christ is about walking in humility, acknowledging wrongdoing, asking for forgiveness, and learning to love completely as we more intimately come to know and mimic the God we serve. I am grateful for the rich truths I have gained and the work that remains before me in the process of my Christian life. Through this book I pray you are able to uncover the mystery in what it is you believe and ultimately who you were made to be.

CHAPTER 1

What is Contentment?

Sharp Discomforts of Uncertainty

Before a search begins, one must know what one is looking for. Before I download an app on my smart phone and start playing Pokémon GO, I had better know what a Pokémon is. And, truthfully, I have no clue what a Pokémon is. These little cartoon characters came on the scene long after my childhood years, and they never caught my daughter's interest. But I'm told that millions of people do know who, or what, a Pokémon is, and they're searching like crazy for these creatures to the point of making national headlines as they blindly walk off cliffs and run into telephone poles. How this is possible, I have no idea. Apparently the game requires staring at your phone while you physically chase this imaginary thing using a GPS — until the two worlds of fantasy and reality collide.

I prefer to look where I'm going. I also like to see adversity coming my way. And if I'm getting a shot or giving blood, I prefer to stare at the needle until it is fully inserted into my arm. I don't like to be stuck and not know when it's coming. That's exactly why getting an epidural ranks at the top of my list of horrible experiences.

When my daughter was born, I was asked to show up for a scheduled C-section with no pain and no clue as to what a contraction felt like. Wearing a gown that exposed half my backside in a chilly, sterile operating room intimidated me enough, but the doctors felt the need to add a needle the size of a cattle prod to the mix. The moment I saw the needle was the exact time I was asked to sit on the table. I tugged at my gown and tried to conceal my backside while I mentally tried to convince myself that obstetricians look at private parts all day long and revealing my birthday suit would be no big deal to them.

While I wrestled on the inside about my vulnerability, masked terrorists unexpectedly came at me with a javelin aimed at my backside, the very piece of property I was trying to protect. There was the problem. I couldn't see behind me. And I don't like sharp surprises, especially ones of that size and nature. Fortunately, a very generous nurse about as tall as she was wide read the look on my face and volunteered to stand in front of me so I could wrap my arms around her in a tight hug before I was jabbed in the back by the epidural. The shell shock of the invasion caused me to go a step beyond the traditional hug, and before I knew what was going on I found my head violently buried in her well-endowed chest. There was my head. Right there in the middle. I believe it was the oddest comfort I've ever received.

One thing is certain...I don't like uncertainty.

Being Certain: Contentment Defined

If we are chasing something and trying to avoid any adverse surprises along the way, then isn't it helpful to be clear on what we are chasing and the best way to catch it? The first logical question to ask is,

"What is contentment?" Being a seasoned student from the school of hard knocks, it would be easier for me to write a dissertation on what contentment is *not*. But I can wipe away the sweat from my brow and put my restless mind at ease knowing that greater minds than my own have been challenged to define this word.

The wisest mind of all time, King Solomon, wrote an entire book (Ecclesiastes) about his quest to find meaning in this life "under the sun." In other words, his pursuit was from an earthly perspective, without consideration of God the Father in Heaven, above the sun. His horizontal perspective revealed one thing after another to be void of meaning. Solomon was profoundly affected by the meaninglessness of life under the sun.

Here's what we know about Solomon:

1. He was wealthy.

   "So King Solomon surpassed all the kings of the earth in riches and wisdom." 1 Kings 10:23

2. He was wise.

   "Then God said to Solomon... 'wisdom and knowledge are granted to you; and I will give you riches and wealth and honor, such as none of the kings have had who were before you, nor shall any after you have the like'."
   2 Chronicles 1:11–12

3. He experienced misery.

   "Therefore I hated life because the work that was done under the sun was distressing to me, for all is vanity and grasping for the wind." Ecclesiastes 2:17

King Solomon was a man with incomparable riches, ruling a vast territory. God said He would pour out riches upon him, and

He did. Scriptures tell us that King Solomon had many houses, orchards, and vineyards, and much livestock. He had many servants and mighty soldiers. His military power was so impressive that he established cities to station his chariots. He established other cities for the sole purpose of storage. We are given a detailed inventory of his wealth, and we are told that silver and gold were as common as stones in Jerusalem.

In addition to having all the stuff he could ever want or need, Solomon was given wisdom superior to that of anyone else on Earth, which made him so famous that all the other kings and queens sought his presence. Solomon's spectacular wisdom not only piqued the interest of other rulers, but they also lavished more riches upon him because of it.

The queen of Sheba came to him with hard questions, and she, like everyone else, was amazed by his greatness.

> "And she gave the king one hundred and twenty talents of gold, spices in great abundance, and precious stones; there never were any spices such as those the queen of Sheba gave to King Solomon." 2 Chronicles 9:9

So how does a man who has this kind of power, prestige, and intellect end up so stinkin' miserable? How did he end up wallowing in it? Why did he feel like everything he had and did was like chasing the wind?

His focus.

Remember, his whole perspective was "under the sun." He didn't have a vertical focus to help him look beyond the earthly tangibles and find his answers. He sought earthly pleasures to fill a void that only God can fill. In fact, Solomon wrote that God has put eternity in our hearts. And that means that there is nothing this earth can offer, whether it be a material possession or a personal relationship, that will *ever* fill the void that only God can fill. He designed us that way.

So if we were hard-pressed to come up with a definition of contentment, under the sun, where would we look? We could use the dictionary, which would attempt to define this word as a "state of happiness and satisfaction," and we would see synonyms like ease, comfort, well-being, and peace.

I don't know about you, but I wrestle with the nonchalant interchangeability of words like happiness and peace. There have been times in my life when I've been *at peace* with a situation that didn't make me *happy*. For instance, I've been at peace with the loss of a loved one who suffered a long-term illness, but did my loss make me *happy*? Was saying good-bye *easy*? I think not.

I'll accept the word *peace*, because I could make a list of lousy experiences where I've found complete peace, whether it be ongoing surgeries on my child, a divorce, or even loss of man's best friend. I can guarantee you that none of those situations put a smile on my face, but the quiet steadiness and strength I felt within did prove to be the power of peace.

My idea of happiness is totally different and has much more of a carefree flair to it. I'm sure I could brainstorm a long list of things I enjoy that make me happy — grinning ear to ear happy. For the sake of discussion, I'll confess that cheeseburgers, chocolate, and theme parks fall on this list, and if you were to combine them all in one delightful experience, you would see me frolicking around like a kid in a candy shop.

Peace and happiness; the two just don't equate. So how do we know what contentment is and whether we've got it, if we can't even properly define what it is?

Actually, we can.

I want to emphasize the difference between absolute and relative truth. You see, it doesn't matter what I think contentment is, because my idea may differ from yours. I could think it's snuggling up with pink and purple polka-dotted puppies with two scoops of vanilla ice cream, while you think it's strategically positioning green army men in formations amid the smell of smoking cannons. It's all relative to *my* point of view, or relative to *your* point of view. Without an anchor, these word games we play are a moving target that we'll never hit. So let's toss any tools "under the sun," including Webster's dictionary. Let's dive deep for the treasure of absolute truth which will surely become our anchor.

What does the word of God, our anchor as Christians, say about contentment? Let's begin with a basic definition of the original Greek word used in the original Scriptures.

Arkeo means
...to be sufficient
...to be possessed of sufficient strength
...to be strong
...to be enough for a thing
...to defend, ward off
...to be satisfied.

I'm already feeling more at ease releasing myself from the idea that the size of a smile plastered across my face is the litmus test measuring my degree of contentedness. This faulty approach assumes happy smiles are the primary indicator of contentment.

Sufficiency.

Strength.

These particular words speak to more boldly to my heart and make more sense to me. However, we also see included in the definition of *arkeo* this notion of defending or warding off. What might that look like? To fully grasp a key to contentment that I missed for years, we need to look at some clues. Using this part of the definition, wouldn't it be reasonable to assume that being on the defensive requires us to be on the lookout, watching for what's coming?

Solomon gives us some wise hints that will help us achieve contentment.

"I returned and saw under the sun that...the sons of men are snared in an evil time." Ecclesiastes 9:11–12

"Thorns and snares are in the way of the perverse; he who guards his soul will be far from them." Proverbs 22:5

One thing most of us can surely agree upon is that hindsight is 20/20. Solomon discovered his lessons the hard way, after sparing no expense and exhausting all earthly pleasures. He saw the futility of trying to be ultimately satisfied by the things of this life. And he was able to reflect upon his meaningless pursuits, boiling it down to these simple statements.

"Let us hear the conclusion of the whole matter: fear God and keep His commandments, for this is man's all. For God will bring every work into judgment, including every secret thing, whether good or evil." Ecclesiastes 12:13–14

Our paths are going to have some briars and thorns. We'll get snagged, and we will have to stop and release ourselves. Rarely does a briar ever break free on its own. It most likely will require some careful picking on our part, and we may flinch when we have to remove it.

Worse than the briars and thorns, our paths are going to be sprinkled with snares and traps, spring-loaded and waiting for unsuspecting victims to step right onto the trigger. It'll probably be a rusty old trap, one that's been around for a while, but it's a trap most effective. Getting out of this bind might cause more than a flinch.

As Solomon learned, there is nothing new under the sun. Satan has used traps like materialism, lust, and greed since the beginning of time, and they still work today. We all fall prey to them. That's why Solomon's wisdom should be heeded when he tells us to guard our souls. Even though Solomon found himself in a few snares, let us not forget that God gave him wisdom like no other, and so the wisdom he dispenses as a result of these experiences should be received.

But what if you don't watch out for the traps? What if you aren't careful in guarding your soul? I can assure you that you're in good company. From time to time, Brer Rabbit fell into a trap, and like him, I have also been a "dumb bunny" that pounced on almost every trigger set before me — enough times that I could write a book about it! As I bounce back down my trail in this story, with 20/20 vision, of course, I can clearly see how I didn't guard myself from those unexpected snares. Consequently, my contentment was snatched and it took a while to get it back. Praise God for coming to the defense of a bound-up creature and graciously setting me free over and over again. I thank Him for teaching me about His freedom and the contentment He wants me to have. My hope for you is to reflect on your path and to learn the same.

CHAPTER 1:

TOOLS FOR DISCOVERY & DISCUSSION

1. How do you define contentment? What do you use as your source or anchor of the definition?

2. If your soul comprises your mind, will, and emotions, then how does the advice King Solomon gave about guarding your soul impact you? Have you considered the many ways we often fail to guard our souls against sin and temptation?

3. Can you think of some "thorns and snares" that have robbed you of your contentment? Have you been freed from these traps or are you still struggling to find lasting satisfaction?

4. Solomon talks about his troubles from a perspective "under the sun" and without regard to God. Would you say that you've searched for contentment using the same perspective?

CHAPTER 1: A SEARCH FOR BIBLICAL TRUTH
GUARDING THE SOUL

Moses addressed the nation of Israel at the end of his life and ministry. As the people gathered to hear him speak, they were reminded of God's covenant with them and the blessings that came with obeying His commands. They were also warned of the curses for not keeping God's covenant. Read this speech in Deuteronomy chapters 29 and 30. What insights do you glean from the conditional covenant in this passage and the significance of the word "if"? What did Moses urge Israel to do in Deuteronomy 30:16?

King Solomon, another great leader of Israel, came face to face with the same choice of obedience. His detour of misery, apart from God and in pursuit of earthly pleasures, led him to ask a particular question in Ecclesiastes 1:2-3. What was his question? Everything seemed so meaningless. After extensive (and expensive) research of the matter, he came to a single conclusion. He concluded the point and purpose to a man's life according to Ecclesiastes 12:13 is what?

The Hebrew word for "keep" in Ecclesiastes 12:13 is the same Hebrew word used in Deuteronomy 30:16. It is also used again in Proverbs 22:5 which has been translated into English (NKJV) as "guards". How do we correlate these three verses and determine the best way to guard our soul and stay in the blessings of God?

CHAPTER 2

Chasing Titles

College

As far as my story is concerned, contentment doesn't arrive on the scene until further down the trail, so we'll make a few stops before we get there. Our first stop isn't exactly starting at square one, but you could say it's number one on the paint-by-numbers plan I had developed for myself upon graduation. Don't we all know what's best for us the moment we shed that cap and gown? It sounds so silly now, but I had meticulously thought out where I'd be and what I'd be doing. Number one: college.

I attended Ole Miss. Red and blue had run through my veins for quite some time, so making my higher education choice was a no-brainer. If you're not from my neck of the woods, you would call it the University of Mississippi.

No, I didn't travel far to get to college, and yes, many times before I have declared that I am a mountain girl, but that's only because of my deep love for climbing a majestic mountain that stretches well above the timberline. As much as I'd love to live in an alpine paradise, the truth is, I live in Mississippi where it's as flat as a flitter and there's nothing to climb except the local water tower.

Yes, I did that too. It wasn't on the paint-by-numbers plan, but sometimes I did color outside the lines. If you've ever watched a toddler color, you are well aware of their distractibility, and such was the case with me. Add a little peer pressure, rebellious inspiration, and a can of green spray paint, and one can quickly cross a line.

I was not under divine inspiration in those days; it was more like being under the inspiration of Billy Bob from the number one song on the country charts — which happened to be about another bright individual climbing a water tower. His sole purpose was to declare his love for Charlene in letters three feet high in John Deere green. I didn't have the same agenda. I just agreed with a few other special people that it was a good idea to paint the water tower.

Although I wasn't declaring my love in that rebellious act, I did know going into college what my declared major would be: Accounting. I took my first accounting course my senior year of high school. It was black and white and made sense to me. Everything had a bucket, a place. I am a firm believer to this day that everything has a place: socks, underwear, keys, mail, you name it. Some things shouldn't be left haphazardly on the floor or mounded on the kitchen table or strategically hidden on top of the armoire where short people like me can't see that it's there, at least not in my ideal house. Furthermore, I have never fully understood how a set of keys can go AWOL on a daily basis. If they have a place, then how can they ever go missing?

This is why accounting worked for me. It was methodical and orderly, and I was in complete control over where everything went. Again, hindsight is 20/20, and it seems there are other methodic fields of study that could have worked for me instead of accounting. I like to build things, so Engineering could have been a good choice too — you know, if I had to do it all over again. Nevertheless, I became a bean counter and used that as the avenue to build something else — my little empire.

I must confess the superficial reason I pursued an accounting degree: money. I felt like I never had much of it, and I wanted to change that. I had met a couple of individuals who were accountants, and their lifestyles looked much different than my own.

Obviously, I still lived under my daddy's roof at the time when this root of greedy discontent sprang up. My daddy worked as a railroad switchman. He didn't work an eight-to-five shift. His job was different. Everything was based on seniority, and the men with the most seniority got to bid on the shifts they wanted to work. They had paid their dues working years of the leftover shifts, so, when the time came, they were quick to choose the eight-to-five, no-travel shift as soon as they could hold it down.

One of the least desirable shifts was called the "extra board," which meant the men would be on call to work any random shifts needing help, usually due to someone calling in sick. The men on the extra board were only guaranteed a few hours of rest before going back on the dispatcher's call list. These were the days before cell phones provided flexibility and convenience, so Daddy would be tied to the landline at home, waiting on his call to go to work. Missing it was not an option, because a missed call could result in being fired.

The extra board seemed to have a lot of available road jobs, so Daddy kept his grip packed at all times. If his shift ended while he was out of town, then he stayed in the local roach motel until the dispatcher called him to work his way back home. And if he happened to make his way back home a day or so later and quitting time was early in the morning, then we had better find something quiet to do so he could collapse in bed and get a few hours of rest during the day. Momma whacked us with many wooden spoons while he slept; she guarded his sleep. In hindsight, we needed it.

It didn't take much effort to notice the differences in lifestyle led by the few accountants I had come across. They drove nice new cars and lived in big homes in *that* part of town. It appeared they worked consistent hours, and they didn't seem to worry about being shipped out of town because they didn't have enough seniority to hold down a regular daylight job in the local yard. I was pretty sure they didn't have to work the graveyard, swing, or any other weird shift that took them out on the rails on every major holiday, in the freezing rain, scorching desert heat, or fiercest tornado winds.

They didn't wear overalls, and they didn't seem to have dark circles and bags under their eyes —because, let's face it, sleeping in the daytime just ain't like sleeping at night. They ate at nice restaurants and didn't look like the type to carry the same lunch pail for decades, eating the same cold, meager offerings paired with a thermos of coffee to get them through the night so they could return home to their loved ones with all limbs still intact.

Daddy sacrificed so much for us during those years. I later realized that he worked all those horrible shifts even when he had earned enough seniority to hold a regular daylight job. Why did he do it? His family. He strategically selected a night job because it gave him the time to be there for us when we got out of school. He wouldn't miss a ballgame of ours if he could possibly avoid it. So he worked stinky hours. He ate monotonous lunches, if that's what you call it at 2 a.m., so that he could still give us a twenty to go out on Saturday night.

He even let me drive his old 1977 Ford Bronco. It was a little embarrassing when I had to roll down the driver's side window and make a "Daisy Duke" exit because the door wouldn't open, but there was something about independence and not having to rely on someone else to cart you around everywhere that made the nuisances fade away. Besides, most people I knew drove old beat up rags too, so I didn't have too much to be embarrassed about. Who cared if the orange stripes didn't run all the way down one of its white panels because it had been wrecked? It got me to where I needed to be.

I remember the gas needle flopping to the left towards "E" every time I hit the gas pedal, and I'd think *there went half my paycheck and an entire weekend of work*. It took wiping down lots of tables and serving countless pots of coffee to the local old timers at 5 a.m. to feed that beast's tank.

No, I didn't have it bad. I just wanted more. Daddy made sure we were provided for, and even though we didn't live in *that* part of town, we did have what we needed. We even had shoes. It was amazing to me that, even though we lived in northern Mississippi where there wasn't much opportunity for work or recreation, the people from the largest neighboring city, Memphis, would often ask if people where we lived wore shoes. I guess in their minds they thought of all Mississippians as poor, uneducated hillbillies.

Not only did Daddy make sure we had shoes, but he also made sure we had family vacations each year. This is where my love for travel and the mountains came from. He would take us out West, and I had seen and experienced just about every national monument and state park west of the Mississippi long before I had read about them in school during Social Studies. We may have dined out of a cooler and slept in the back of the truck or in a tent, but they were memories that no one could put a price tag on.

By the time I reached high school, I wanted more. Something in me stirred, and I wanted my adult life to be a *little* richer than that of my childhood. I wanted what *they* had. So I began my studies in accounting to see if I could make that happen.

Now don't think for one second that my college experience was strait-laced and all about the studies. I discovered a whole new world out there, one where the party was the pulse that kept me feeling alive. The pinnacle of an Ole Miss Rebel's social gathering was The Grove on game day.

The Grove was famous for its majestic oaks towering above a lush green lawn. It created a shady canopy in the center of campus where one could peacefully sprawl out on a blanket mid-week as the squirrels scurried in every direction. On game day, The Grove transformed to tailgate central. All the tents, cram-packed together, made it look like a refugee camp, except it was anything but a refugee camp.

There were no starving third-world refugees in this place. If anyone was starving, it was their own fault because the amount of fried chicken forked out of these tents on the finest china, and all of the other delectable Southern dishes proudly presented on the pottery of notorious Mississippi Delta craftsmen, was enough to feed a small country. The food was art. Its scents lingered in the air. It was game day. And no expense was spared.

Also on game day, student tradition required proper attire. The men wore ties, and the women looked like they just walked out of Saks Fifth Avenue. It was like the Kentucky Derby on steroids, minus the hats. Women pranced around The Grove in heels until it was time to go to the stadium. Once the game started, all the students stood in their section the entire time with the high probability that cocktails would be spilled on their backs by intoxicated Rebel peers swaying from behind. On this day, a sea of rebel flags were dancing across Vaught-Hemingway Stadium, the melody of Dixie was playing, smoky cannons were firing, and, of course, the chant of "Hotty Toddy" was filling the air.

There came a point when we women couldn't feel our feet anymore, thanks to the bourbon, and we were sauced up enough to think it was a good idea to walk at least another mile, in heels, to the post-game party. There, we could wrap up the night with an apartment complex of other rednecks who would sing, in unison, the anthem of the party, David Allan Coe's *You Never Even Called Me by My Name*. Tradition. Who cares if it makes sense, right?

My favorite t-shirt in college read "Ole Miss, we're not snobs..." on the front and "we're just better than you" on the back. This summed it up. And it's what I believed.

It was a miracle my scholarship dollars didn't go to waste. And it's a miracle that the person I describe sounds like a complete stranger to me. I was proud. Smug. And devious as the day was long. My relationships were bound together like a strand of paper dolls, and were just as easily broken if I didn't get what I wanted. One by one, I severed relationships as I selfishly fulfilled my desires. My moral deviation and downward spiral blinded me to the damage and pain I caused a lot of people.

Graduation came and went, and I was all about the title. It was a fascination that fueled my ego. I had been Salutatorian of my high school class and received enough scholarships to pay for my entire college education. Despite being intoxicated with liquid spirits, and with myself, I somehow managed to graduate from college with honors, too. Job offers from several major accounting firms in Memphis sat on my desk awaiting my decision prior to finishing my graduate degree. Pride fed my pursuit of *more* and further disconnected me from my humble roots.

Career

I took one of the job offers in Memphis upon graduation, and I was aware that I needed the next title if I was going to pursue a lasting career at the public accounting firm. I had to pass the CPA exam. My superiors displayed their distinguished certificates on the walls of their offices, and they made it clear that if I wanted to advance up the corporate ladder, I, too, would need to obtain a certificate. Okay, challenge accepted.

Sounded easy, but I had to pass a little test to get that certificate and the honor of putting three little initials behind my name. It was the only test I ever took that brought me to tears. After the first day of the exam, salty silent streams stained my face at the thought of having to complete a miserable second day of rigorous test questions for eight solid hours. One guy was carried out on a stretcher during exam day, chest pains I suppose. I thought for sure I'd be next.

No, I didn't pass it the first time. Or the second time. Or even the third time. Or the fourth. (*Sigh.*) Talk about eating humble pie. I had six months to chew on every bitter bite before taking my next serving. Since the exam was only given twice a year, I was forced to wait and agonize over the next scheduled test date.

Waiting on scores to arrive in the mailbox weeks after filling in hundreds of bubbles on the exam paper was torture for someone who was antsy to get this title under her belt. But when I finally received a passing grade on all four parts of the exam, I was one happy girl.

Did the satisfaction of my new prestige last? Of course not. It was just a matter of housekeeping so I could press on toward my goal. And at the time, a reasonable goal was to get promoted so I could finally have a real office with a door and a view instead of a padded cubicle next to the guy who had perfect potential to go postal and fire off a few rounds.

Getting promoted wasn't a given, though. Strict evaluations came and went, and I discovered there was much I didn't know, things that weren't taught in school. It was up to my supervisor to teach me the ropes. However, I came to the stark realization that many of them either didn't want us to succeed, or weren't interested in babysitting and training new hires. In-charge accountants raced a clock to complete every job in budgeted time. Therefore, it hit me that training staff took time that managers didn't have. Even if they did have the time to train and do it well, helping a less experienced staff person move up through the ranks could jeopardize their spot on the ladder or, worse, cut into their piece of the pie when it came to sharing profits and bonuses.

Reality Check

Only one year into my career at the firm, I felt like I had seen enough to know that I was cut from a different bolt of fabric. That was not what I wanted to do for the rest of my life, but there was one small problem. I didn't have the experience needed to jump ship and go somewhere else in private industry. And I sure wasn't going back to school and admitting I had made a mistake in my choice of profession. I was committed until that next door of opportunity swung open. I didn't enjoy coding every day in incremental time slots, including my bathroom breaks. I didn't enjoy being enslaved by tax season demands. And I didn't enjoy being bored with the work that

I was doing. I felt trapped, but I kept pushing the paper for a paycheck.

I tried to learn as much as I could while I was at the firm, and I found that one of the most interesting parts of being an auditor was having manufacturing clients. I loved to see each client's unique process of manufacturing, and I often marveled at the ingenuity behind creating a product. However, having manufacturing clients meant that they had inventory, and inventory had to be counted. It was part of my job to perform an objective inventory count on the last day of their fiscal year.

One of my clients milled dog food, and they had a normal December 31 calendar year end. Their milling plant was located on President's Island, out on the Mississippi River, and I had to inspect their raw materials, which smelled like death. The inspection involved climbing a silo that rose up into the frigid, gray winter skies. Good thing I had experience climbing ridiculously tall objects. Apparently Billy Bob's water tower wasn't a waste of time. Every rung of that cold metal ladder reminded me of the irony of my situation.

The irony lay in the fact that I had striven to have a job that looked nothing like my daddy's, but there I was, down in the same industrial yard on New Year's Day, working while most people were off and snuggled warm in their beds. My ears almost snapped off in the cold as I climbed silos and walked along a mile of boxcars in the loose gravel. It was also part of my job to ensure that the rail cars containing inventory were accurately reported. I could have sworn that the rail cars amplified the bite of the wind as it bounced off the rusty frames and straight through my coat. All of a sudden, Daddy's quilted Carhartt® bibbed overalls didn't sound so bad.

On the other end of the spectrum, a different client owned sister companies that mined gravel and paved asphalt roads. Their fiscal year ended in the heat of summer, and they owned many gravel pits across North Mississippi. Again, it was my job to count the inventory. I spent an entire day going from pit to pit and stepping the perimeter of each mountain of crushed rock, estimating how many tons lay in that pile. I smelled like a gorilla by the end of the day, as the sun bore down on me and wrung any trace of my morning shower from my body. Again, irony.

I had believed the first step of my paint-by-numbers plan would surely bring contentment, but it wasn't panning out that way. I wasn't the happy little toddler who had just finished coloring in all the "number one" shapes, proudly proclaiming, "Look what I did!" Rather, I was being nagged by an inner grumbling of dissatisfaction with my career.

Too proud to take ownership of my choices and too caught up in playing the part, I found myself in the twin snares of pride and greed. I was proudly chasing the almighty dollar, and I didn't even recognize it.

CHAPTER 2:

TOOLS FOR DISCOVERY & DISCUSSION

1. Can you retrace your steps and determine whether you began to pursue something for the wrong reasons? What was the rationale for your pursuit?

2. Is there anything from your cultural upbringing that caused you to go in a particular direction? What thoughts, beliefs, and feelings instigated you to travel this particular path?

3. How have pride and greed affected your life? What relationships, if any, have suffered or been severed at the hands of these snares?

CHAPTER 2: A SEARCH FOR BIBLICAL TRUTH

GOD'S PURSUIT OF OUR HEARTS

Living in bondage of our past is not healthy. What does Galatians 5:1 say about bondage? We were not meant to be held as slaves and prisoners of our past. However, there are benefits from looking into our past like learning how patterns and behaviors have developed and understanding how those behaviors affect our present, and potentially, our future. It takes courage to ask the hard questions of self-examination and even more so, to tell the truth about what we discover. What did David write in Psalm 139:23-24? Are you willing for God to search your heart on this journey?

What does Ecclesiastes 3:11 say that God put in our hearts? What did Jesus say in John 6:40? He said it's God's will for "everyone" to have everlasting life. If God places eternity in our hearts and desires for everyone to have a relationship with Him, then what does He do? Read John 6:44. He draws us near to Jesus. Who does He draw near? Everyone (John 6:40). Again, that is His will. If you do not have a personal relationship with Jesus, have you considered the probing questions in this book as His means of pursuing you to begin a loving relationship with Him?

CHAPTER 3

Chasing the American Dream

Chasing titles and, ultimately, a dollar wasn't the only thing driving me. Like a dog spinning in circles trying to sink its teeth into its own tail, I chased the American Dream, which seemed to be the next phase of my plan. It was an endless chase as I dragged around the weight and chains of the first two snares and haphazardly stumbled into new ones.

I was engaged to be married during spring break of my senior year at Ole Miss. Like any bride, I had dreams of what the perfect wedding would look like. I had stacks of bridal magazines and a planning portfolio bursting at the seams, documenting every little detail. I could see in my mind what I wanted it to look like, so my search for the perfect gown, the perfect venue, the perfect flowers, and the perfect day commenced.

It was a lot of pomp and circumstance. After all, it was *my* day. And that's what I wanted: it had to be all about me. All eyes would be fixed on me as I walked down a really long aisle with a really long train. I don't recall asking whether my choices worked for anyone else — my bridesmaids, my parents, or even the groom.

All of the bridesmaids' dresses would coordinate perfectly, even though the style of dress I chose didn't complement the variety of body types standing next to me. The same bodies who generously footed the bill for a dress they'd never wear again. I'm sure I could have qualified for the Bridezilla show, because I recall getting angry with one of my best friends for getting a barbed-wire tattoo that wrapped around her biceps days before my event. How dare she do such a thing, exposing a tattoo that didn't even match the dresses at *my* wedding!

How dare the florists bring the wrong kind of flowers, ones that didn't come close to comparing with the ones I had ordered, and which, like the tattoo, didn't coordinate with the bridesmaids' dresses?

How dare the music coordinator, who had generously volunteered his time, mix up the sequence of songs, so that I was left still trying to light the unity candle when the music ended? The awkward silence was embarrassing.

I'm telling you, I could have found a flaw with Jesus Himself. But I wasn't too terribly focused on Him, because it was *my* day. Oh, I played the part and said some shallow prayers during the ceremony, but it was really all about me. I was more concerned with pageantry than with spiritual covenants.

My parents sacrificed a chunk of retirement savings to make my day possible. In all of my self-absorption, I failed to consider that the year I married was the year of their twenty-fifth wedding anniversary. Instead of celebrating their accomplishment by taking the honeymoon they never had or throwing a party for themselves, they poured their funds into my celebration. I accepted it without reservation and without even acknowledging their milestone or sacrifice.

College degree, check.

Diamond ring — I mean, marriage, check.

Job, check.

What's next on the list? A home, of course.

Isn't the apex of the American Dream owning a home with a white, picket fence? As much as I wanted to immediately start out in a brand new home, we ended up spending our first year renting a townhome while I finished college.

The townhome had dark brown shag carpet, and the tenant who lived there prior to us had cats that left behind talons and other undesirable artifacts. I thought all cats knew how to find a litter box, but I have to assume that either there was no litter box or the tenant neglected to change it.

Our carpet wasn't the only thing wild about the apartment complex. We had a neighbor about our age, and she liked to have guests over frequently, many of whom ended up staying the night. The uninsulated cinderblock walls that separated our apartment bedroom from hers revealed quite a bit about her, and we wondered if she had any clue that her private activities echoed over into our space. We lay in bed many nights bug-eyed with shock and unable to sleep for all the commotion. Come morning, when we headed to our cars to start the day, we often exited our apartments at the same time, and we would grin slyly at her, because surely she thought all her secrets were safe.

Our landlord was a different kind of colorful. She was also a bit of a slumlord, because when our rusty old hot-water heater burst and filled the downstairs with water, soaking everything we owned, she thought it was acceptable to rip out the smelly carpet, drape it over the dumpster to dry, and reinstall it in our apartment. I just about had a fit. Although the brown shag hid whatever the landlord wasn't able to clean out of the carpet, the underneath exposed the serious-ness of the moldy stains and the truth about the cats. The landlord finally conceded to my demands and replaced the carpet downstairs. She installed the cheapest, bright pink carpet she could find, which violently clashed with the remaining brown shag going up the stair-well, but I didn't care because it was brand new and it was the only carpeted space in the apartment on which I felt comfortable walking barefoot.

I don't know exactly what I expected to get for $300 a month, but I was hoping for more than she was willing to offer. So I was thrilled when we moved out of the townhome and into our brand-new, two-bedroom, zero-lot-line starter home. It was a place I could walk barefoot and not worry about contracting worms or being stabbed by a claw. The neighbors were a little less entertaining, but we were able to get more peaceful sleep. Since we were "moving on up" (like the Jeffersons), I took pride in taking care of the house and putting our personal touches on it.

However, over the years I've discovered that the problem with having *things* is that it perpetuates a need to keep on buying other things. The house was no different. I had this beautiful new house, but the landscaping needed some attention. Since we bought the house in December, every bush on the property looked dead, and half of them didn't come to life in the spring. It looked plain to me, and even though I had never owned anything quite so fantastic before, I still wanted it to be better. Oh, isn't that how *Better Homes and Gardens* and *Southern Living* and a myriad of other home improvement entities make their fortunes? People just like me who get sucked into having a picture-perfect showcase home.

It only seemed prudent to scour my magazines for the next home improvement project that our paychecks would allow. Each time a new issue arrived in my mailbox, I'd rip off the plastic and feast my eyes on a lengthy list of luxurious ideas I should apply to my home.

All of a sudden, the quaint, hand-me-down furniture that perfectly met all my needs, carried me through college, and survived the townhome flood wasn't good enough. I didn't want those raggedy old pieces in the brand new home. They didn't fit. They didn't look anything like the pictures in the magazines, so I was able to make a convincing case that we needed to go furniture shopping. I didn't like the idea of financing the furniture, especially after signing on the dotted lines at our mortgage closing and seeing how much we would *really* pay for that little house after thirty years. But I justified the purchase: the credit was available and, bottom line, I wanted it.

I also wanted a new car. I had sworn to myself that this would not be a purchase I'd make as soon as I graduated and landed a good job, but shifting gears every day during stop-and-go rush hour in pantyhose and heels, and with a failing air conditioner, made the commute uncomfortable and had me second-guessing my resolution. Not to mention the fact that my truck leaked oil, and an oil stain was developing on the concrete parking pad in front of the new home. It didn't complement the lush green lawn I had worked so hard to perfect. Like the house and the furniture, I justified needing a new car. And like the house and the furniture, I failed to negotiate a reasonable price. I was the easiest sell ever.

"Here's the over-inflated price, ma'am."

"Okay, let me get my checkbook!" I chirped as I hop-skipped into the sunset.

It only took a few chuckles from friends and a few months of bills flooding the mailbox before I realized that I had been an idiot in not even attempting to negotiate a better deal. I was angry with myself for being so reckless, so I declared that I would drive the expensive four-wheel-drive Toyota 4-Runner until the wheels fell off.

The vehicle was no different from the house; it needed expensive add-ons like insurance, annual registration, and license plates. It also required, in my mind, upgraded accessories like floor mats, bug guards, and vent visors. After all, this vehicle was my ticket to enjoying the great outdoors in luxury and style.

Now that I had a vehicle to take me up the mountains or wherever I wanted to go, the versatility of my new ride and my love for travel instigated another purchase. When we travel, I thought to myself, we would need a place to stay. What better way to do it than to have a piece of property that's paid for. So I justified signing a mortgage on another piece of property — a timeshare.

Time would soon show how unwise that decision was. Vacation club dues, taxes, and high maintenance fees on a property that was seldom available when we wanted it became a heavy burden. And I was dumb enough to buy two of them! Fortunately, I was able to talk someone into taking one of them off my hands. I don't know why I ever thought a timeshare could be considered an investment.

New house.

Improved landscaping.

New furniture.

New car.

New vacation property.

These were my newfound possessions. They were perks of a salary from a career I didn't even enjoy. And, like every other thing that came before them, they didn't provide lasting satisfaction. They left me wanting more.

I found myself sitting in a house full of new stuff that needed to be paid for, so I pushed my spouse to get a better job. Going against the advice of my dad, we considered him interviewing for a position at the railroad. Even though I knew the risks and challenges that lifestyle presented, the perks of a solid paycheck and strong benefits appealed to me, so I urged him to go forward with it. After all, I had grown up around railroaders, and going back to that lifestyle wouldn't be too hard. For me, at least. I wasn't going to be the one out on the rails in the worst of conditions.

As expected, he got stuck working the night shift, as well as weekends and holidays. He was always gone. The house began to feel empty. My new couch didn't talk to me. Nor did the 4-Runner. And although the house didn't say it out loud, there always seemed to be an unspoken "clean me." That was not the company I longed for. I do appreciate a sparkly clean toilet, but any time spent with it didn't feel like quality time.

Something was still missing. I was too footloose and fancy-free to want to care for a baby at that point, so starting a family was not on my radar. The thought of it actually terrified me. So I reasoned that the next best thing would be getting a dog. At least if I was horrible at mothering and accidentally killed it, I would not be hauled off to jail. I had managed to kill a cactus before, so I wanted to take baby steps when it came to being responsible for another living, breathing thing.

This is when I met my first little fur baby. Actually, like Mowgli, I grew up with a pack of dogs, so technically this was not my first dog. But he would be my very own, my first since becoming a responsible adult and moving out of my parents' house.

A friend connected me with a family that was getting rid of some black lab pups. The pups already had their shots, and that was the only cost I had to cover to call one mine. They didn't have registered papers, but, for once, a title didn't seem to matter to me. There was no question: he was full-blooded and as cute as a bug's ear.

I never before had a dog as big as a Labrador Retriever, and I couldn't wait to get my hands on him. Before I went to see the litter, I was instructed to pick a puppy that wasn't hyper, one that seemed calm. So I did. I chose my sweet little Cotton. He was black as night, but the irony of his having a name representing something opposite his color seemed funny to us. Like naming the scrawny, runt-of-the-litter pup "Tank." Cotton immediately put a twinkle in my eye. He was my new best friend, and it wasn't long before I couldn't remember what life was like before having him around. A life of clean toilets and silent furniture?

It also wasn't long before I realized the calm demeanor he displayed the night we met was all a pretentious act. Perhaps he had just eaten and was so full he couldn't move. I don't know. But that dog had more energy than we knew what to do with. His hind legs were faster than his front legs, and it would tickle the fire out of me to watch him zoom around the coffee table like a greyhound at the dog track, with his front legs trying their best to stay ahead of his hind legs. In an instant, he'd be in another room, circling something else on his way back towards me. You couldn't catch him. Especially if he snagged a dirty sock out of the laundry pile and you tried to retrieve it. It became a game to him, and good luck getting it back before you had an air-conditioned hole for your big toe!

Cotton was incredibly easy to house train, and he never chewed any furniture, so that was a plus. But he liked to dig holes and run away, and there was no fence around our back yard to contain him. You got it! That was our next major purchase: a fence. I was tired of Cotton walking me with the leash, dragging me down the road, so I reasoned that getting the fence would save wear and tear on my ligaments.

It wasn't long after getting the fence that we were buying bags of concrete mix to fill in the holes along the bottom of the fence that Cotton used to taunt the little dog next door. It was funny watching the little dog pop his head over into our back yard, but after a while I longed to play whack-a-mole with him. He only encouraged Cotton's digging, and the back yard was so pitted that it looked like it had been hit by a meteor shower.

All of these things were my notion of the American Dream, and I believed they would bring me contentment. Like the dog chasing his own tail, I finally caught the dream. But was the dream pulling me, or was I pulling the dream? Without a doubt, keeping up appearances and trying to design my home like the ones in the magazines had a hold on me, and keeping up with the Joneses became very important; I felt as if I had to prove my worth to the world through my possessions.

Sure, these things aren't inherently bad. They did bring happiness and some sense of fulfillment. But it didn't last. It was only a matter of time before the fascia boards began to rot, scratches and dents appeared on the 4-Runner, the furniture broke down, and the timeshare continued to be a money pit.

And because the satisfaction in these things did *not* last, the loss of that feeling of satisfaction would always send me searching for the next best thing. And I'd quickly take care of it. I was in another snare: one of self-sufficiency. This snare was very similar to the first one (greed), in the sense that it revolved around money and making an impression, but this one went a step further and denied any reliance on Jesus.

We both had good paying jobs and a list of new stuff to show for it. If something broke, we fixed it. If we were hungry, we went to the store. If we were sick, our first-class insurance paid our medical bills. Whatever we needed, our paychecks provided. Our self-reliance puffed us up to the point where we believed we could take care of anything that came our way. We were living the American Dream, and had no idea that the illusion of "security" that our comfortable earthly nest provided was about to be picked apart by God's providential hand.

CHAPTER 3:

TOOLS FOR DISCOVERY & DISCUSSION

1. Has chasing the American Dream and keeping up with the Joneses ever caused a chain reaction of purchases in your life that you later regretted? Do you think pursuing bigger and better things is wrong? Why or why not?

2. How has envy of others influenced your behaviors and choices?

3. In what ways has self-sufficiency affected you and your faith? Has a lack of financial resources ever forced you to ask God or others for help?

CHAPTER 3: A SEARCH FOR BIBLICAL TRUTH
THE GREATEST GIFT TO PURSUE

Does God love for His children to receive gifts? Of course,
He does. Read James 1:17 & Matthew 7:11. However, God's
concern for the purity and motives of our hearts, as it pertains to
pursuing material goods, is always going to take precedence over
haphazardly granting any of our personal wish lists. First, He wants
our hearts to be right with Him.

At the end of chapters 1 and 2 we discussed how God pursues
us to have a relationship with Him and instructs us to keep His
commandments. We are reminded in Deuteronomy 30:17-18
that "if" our hearts turn away from Him we are deserving of death.
Everyone has a choice.

Read Romans 1:18-32. In verse 25 Paul wrote that they
"exchanged the truth of God for the lie." What was God's
response in verses 26 and 28 for their unrighteous pursuits? God
is patient, but eventually He gave them over to the unclean things
they pursued. Do you see covetousness, envy, and pride in the list
of unfitting things they sought? How does this affect you as you
self-examine whether these traits are in your own life?

What does Romans 3:23 say about you and me? Our sins may
include envy of others and pride, and our daily choices and
behaviors may not always honor God, but there is still hope. Read
Romans 6:23. What promise follows the "but"? The ultimate gift
to ever be received is the gift of Christ. Our decision to follow
Him is the one choice we must approach most carefully. There

are only two options: accept or reject Him. This matter of the heart was never designed to be complicated. Read Romans 10:13 and take note of the two commands given in Mark 1:15 to understand the simplicity of salvation in Christ: repent and believe.

CHAPTER 4

God's Wake-Up Call

After being married for five years, settling into our home, and proving to ourselves that we were competent enough to keep Cotton alive, we felt we were ready to start a family. Actually, I wasn't that eager to become a parent, having recalled my irresponsibility with the cactus. I wouldn't have minded procrastinating another five years, but my spouse's clock was ticking a little faster than mine, so I agreed it was time. I had convinced myself that it would take about a year to get pregnant and then another nine months for the baby to incubate, and that would buy me some time, about a year and a half, to warm up to the idea of having a little one.

Hurricane Elvis

A straight-line wind storm came out of nowhere on that strange day in July. I don't recall even the first drop of rain with the storm, just violent winds that snapped trees like toothpicks, as if a tornado had barreled through and destroyed the entire city.

I remember peering out the window into the back yard as Cotton's metal dog bowl nearly punctured a hole in the wooden fence as it hurtled across the yard like a flying saucer. The sky was yellow but there were no funnel clouds. It was bizarre. They named this oddity Hurricane Elvis because we lived in the Memphis area, which was once the home of Elvis Presley. I don't know why Elvis's memory was attached to such a destructive storm, but that's what they called it.

I quickly learned of all the streets that were blocked by fallen trees, and I was given permission to stay home rather than reporting to work since there was no power anyway. I was walking across the living room, just getting off the phone with my manager, when something hit me like a bolt of lightning. And just as fast as it hit me, it left.

I stood, motionless, wondering what spurred the instantaneous nausea, and then the thought struck me like Hurricane Elvis. It frightened me far worse than the straight-line winds had. My spouse ran to the corner Walgreens to pick up some tests to confirm our suspicions. Meanwhile, I lay in bed, white as a sheet, staring at the ceiling and shoving saltines into my mouth, oblivious to the crumbs falling into the bed.

Yes, the test was positive. The lie I had told myself about having an eighteen-month buffer reeled in my mind. I wasn't prepared for how sudden this all came about. But I quickly warmed up to the idea.

It didn't take long to agree on a baby name. In fact, the baby name was chosen long before we found out we would be parents. Both the first and middle names we chose could be applied to either gender, so we didn't have to worry about picking multiple names. While I was still in college and before I got married, I lived in an apartment above a single mom and her daughter. The little girl was about four years old, and she melted my heart every day with her prissy little dresses and her grown-up mannerisms like carrying a purse and making sure her blonde, bobbed haircut was perfectly in place as she walked gracefully to and from their apartment. We always said we wanted a little girl, and we would name her after this little girl. The middle name was taken from a grandparent whom I greatly respected and adored. Grandaddy was happy we chose to honor him this way.

Sugar and Spice with a Twist of Lemon

I was still preoccupied with having a perfect home, so the second bedroom needed a change of décor. I picked out paint chips and nursery themes for either gender. And when it was time to find out if I was having a boy or girl, I took the paint chips with me. That is how I was going to break the news to my mom, who was anxiously sitting in the waiting room.

In my heart, I most wanted to have a girl, but I was going to be perfectly happy with a boy, too. I could see myself with either one. I just wanted the suspense to end. I wanted to know who was growing inside of me.

I was tickled *pink* when I learned that I was going to have a little girl. There just aren't enough words to describe the elation of bringing a child into this world. I was on an emotional high for about a week with the excitement of it all. I was fat and happy, and nothing could have dampened my spirit.

Except one phone call.

I was sitting at my desk, the same padded cubicle that reminded me I wasn't going to be promoted to a corner office with windows any time soon. My office phone rang, and I answered. My doctor's office was calling to discuss the results of the triple-screen blood test I had taken a few weeks earlier. It was an optional test that most insurance companies didn't cover, but, fortunately, my insurance did, so I took it.

I sat confused, squinting at the gray walls of my cube as I jotted down unfamiliar words like "neural tube defect" and "perinatologist." I struggled to understand what they meant while the nurse briefly described all that the test results could imply. I was told that a neural tube defect could be several things, and most likely it would be Down's syndrome or spina bifida. I knew what Down's was, but I had no idea what spina bifida was.

Something was wrong. In that instant, my world came crashing down around me.

And it was this moment, right here with this phone call, when God began to clearly intervene in my life. I was not in control, and I was keenly aware of it. In a stupor, I walked over to a friend's office. My friend, thankfully, had been promoted to an office with a window, and, more important, a door.

My friend and his wife had just traveled a similar road when they had their daughter about nine months before. They had also received an unpleasant phone call from their doctor and learned that their daughter would be born with trisomy-18, a different kind of genetic defect. They were living a heart-wrenching story with their daughter, who was not expected to live past a year. They were familiar with the terms that the doctor's office used and the emotions aroused by them. Better than that, they were Christian believers. God strategically placed them in my path so that they could walk alongside me in this painful discovery.

The office door closed, and I sobbed. I fell apart. My friend called his wife and put her on speaker-phone as they told me what to expect in the days ahead as I went through a string of doctors' appointments.

The doctors' appointments that followed were to clarify what was causing the birth defect. I was only eighteen weeks pregnant when they finally found the lesion on her tiny spine with the ultrasound. That lesion indicated that my daughter had spina bifida, and I quickly learned that a lot of scary things came with this condition. The doctors painted a dreary picture; none of them gave me any hope. In fact, they offered me the option of an abortion, suggesting that termination might be the best choice because she most likely would never walk, talk, or have quality of life.

I was in a fog. Just days ago, I was picking out pink nursery accessories. And then I got a phone call and learned that it could all be over.

I was desperate. I needed answers, but I had none. I wish I could tell you that I never considered the abortion, but that wouldn't be the truth. I did consider it — for a moment — because my trusted doctors and specialists all seemed to think it was a reasonable option, perhaps the best option. They didn't offer their opinions and say those exact words. They didn't have to. Their failure to offer any hope and the somber looks on their faces said it for them.

I realized for the first time that none of my perceived self-sufficiency could buy my way to having a healthy baby. This situation was far bigger than me, and there was only one thing I could do: pray. As I prayed, God reminded me of a verse I was familiar with.

> "The effective, fervent prayer of a righteous man avails much." James 5:16

I had never really felt the need to pray with such urgency and fervency as I did in that moment. I had asked the Lord to give me a sign because my faith was so weak that it was going to take a sign for me to see His hand in this situation. I just wanted a doctor to tell me what to do. And, so far, no one was willing to take that risk.

We had one weekend to decide whether to abort or keep our baby, because I was far enough along in the pregnancy that a partial-birth abortion would have to be performed. That could be done only in a neighboring state, and my gestational clock was ticking so rapidly that I was about to cross the threshold where it was no longer an option even in that state.

I had never heard of a partial-birth abortion and was advised by friends to steer clear of the horrors presented on the internet, but I had to understand what the procedure would entail. I logged on, and it took only a moment before I knew: the very thought of it disgusted me.

I felt in my heart that the doctors couldn't be right about my daughter. I had seen her on the ultrasound, moving her arms and legs while I lay on the table and the doctors talked — insensitively —about her lemon-shaped head and all the fluid collected in the ventricles of her brain. When I brought her moving limbs to their attention, they quickly dismissed it, declaring that any movement was caused by the amniotic fluid. I didn't argue with them, but I knew the amniotic fluid never kicked me in the belly like she had. She could move. I was convinced of it. I couldn't convince them of it, but it didn't matter, because the decision was mine to make.

Nevertheless, I still wasn't certain that keeping her would be the best option. It didn't seem *fair* to bring her into this world with the odds against her. I wrestled with the doctors' "no quality of life" comment. Although I had not made a firm decision, I simply knew I didn't want to have an abortion.

My spouse and I didn't speak of it all weekend. The turmoil in my heart and pretending nothing was wrong ate me alive. Thoughts of what it would be like to have a funeral and bury a child haunted me. I had recently begun listening to Christian music on the radio, and the song *Remember Me* by Mark Schultz made me think of my daughter. When I listened to this song, a barrage of questions pounded through my mind. How could I consciously decide to bury my child? Only vividly colored Gerbera daisies would seem fitting for the tiny casket of a baby girl, because they are bright and fun, and that is what my whole week with her was like once I knew that she was, in fact, a girl. How could anyone ever make it through a funeral like that? What would life be like without her after all of this was over? Monday morning came, the day we had agreed to finalize our decision after meeting with one last specialist, a pediatric neurosurgeon. I had prayed for clarity, a sign — and God delivered.

When we told the neurosurgeon the details of the past week and that no one had offered us any hope, he looked dumbfounded. He took a pen from his white coat pocket and began to draw a bell curve with passion and purpose on the crunchy paper covering the examination table. He proceeded to explain the percentage of children with spina bifida who fell in the normal to above average range of cognitive functioning. When we told him most doctors had implied that we should have an abortion, he plainly stated, "That would be a foolish thing to do. Some of the most blessed children in this world are children with disabilities."

That instant I *knew* God had answered my prayer and had given us a doctor who was not only bold enough to tell us the truth, but was skilled enough to fix my daughter's problem! Tears welled in my eyes as he walked us through the procedures he would follow to surgically close the opening in her spine. Then he addressed the fluid in the ventricles of her brain, a condition called "hydrocephalus." He explained what caused it, and told us that it could also be fixed with surgery that would place a shunt in her ventricles. But before we would ever cross that bridge, he insisted I have a C-section because of her hydrocephalus. His concern was to not put any more pressure on her head than necessary. These complex procedures were far beyond my understanding, but he spoke with confidence, and his head full of grey hair set my mind at ease.

When God answers prayers, He answers them fully. This was no exception. He gave us a neurosurgeon whose controlled demeanor resolved my mental chaos, and his calculated patience restored balance to a situation that felt out of control. I appreciated his "let's wait and see" approach when it came to all the uncertainties regarding my daughter's care. And as time went on, I learned to appreciate that aspect of his character even more as we dealt with some of his colleagues, who were far too eager to recommend surgery for my child.

My joy was restored, and my pink preparations resumed. I was more excited than ever, because not only did I have the hope and dream of my little girl back, but now I also had a cool "God moment" to share with everyone. I knew she was special. And I knew that, for some reason, God thought I was special, too, because He chose me to be her mother.

My love for her exploded, even though she was a person I had never seen or touched. And I have to say that God's love towards me surpassed what I felt for her. His love inexplicably wrapped me up like a warm blanket. I felt it, and He was also a person I had never seen or touched. I certainly didn't deserve to be loved like that, but the intimacy of these truths rekindled my passion for Him, and set in motion a series of trials and teaching moments that would continue to draw me closer to Him.

I began to learn some valuable lessons, the elementary building blocks of true faith.

I was *not* in control.

I had *not* given proper attention to my relationship with Him.

I had *not* relied on Him.

I began to realize that my faith was weak, and I pondered some probing questions. Did I love God as much as I loved all my possessions that had captured my attention and affection before this situation arose? Would my love for Him explode as it had for the child He had so graciously given me?

God had caught my attention, and His intervention in my life demanded a response.

CHAPTER 4:

TOOLS FOR DISCOVERY & DISCUSSION

1. Are there any defining moments when you felt God was trying to get your attention?

2. In what instances have you discovered that you were not in control? How did this make you feel? Did fear of not being in control overwhelm you?

3. Have you ever examined your relationship with God? How might your relationship with Him need attention?

CHAPTER 4: A SEARCH FOR BIBLICAL TRUTH

GOD'S DISCIPLINE

In chapter 3, we talked about the simplicity of salvation and how to become a believer in Christ. Read Hebrews 12:1-11. What is one way to discern if you are child of God? Discipline. What does verse 8 say? My friend, if the trials begin to flood your path, it may be cause for a celebration. "Why do you say that?!" you might ask. Because God tends to His children.

Often there are times when God's children who are secure in their salvation make poor choices. Verse 1 instructs us to "lay aside every weight, and the sin which so easily ensnares us." That's not easy to do, especially if we aren't intentionally pursuing holiness and aware of our sin. Rest assured, our Father does not want us to stay in sin, particularly a sin that hooks us every time! So, as any good parent would do, the Lord steps in and disciplines His children. Who does the Lord discipline according to verse 6? We shouldn't despise God's discipline as told in verse 5. Why? Because verse 10 assures us that discipline is for our benefit. Our struggles certainly won't feel joyful, but if you are His child, then there's a good probability that God is allowing it to teach you the peaceable fruit of righteousness. Be encouraged as He loves and trains His children.

CHAPTER 5

Releasing to The Lord

As the Lord drew me nearer in the following months, I realized what a blessing it was to have had the optional blood test done and to know in advance about the defect. I thanked Him time and time again because this knowledge gave my inner planner ample time to coordinate with the doctors and insurance companies.

What if I had *not* known about my daughter's spina bifida or hydrocephalus and had discovered it only upon delivery? Talk about spoiling a moment! I would have been devastated. I was thankful that I had the time to emotionally process and embrace what was to come. After we met with the neurosurgeon for the first time and encountered the Lord in such a mighty way, I was steadfast in believing that no matter how challenging the situation became, God would carry us through it.

Shortly after that meeting with the neurosurgeon, I met with a renowned perinatologist. I was told that he was one of the best in his field. My loved ones asked if I wanted company at this appointment, but I was so spiritually charged that I declined. I said I could handle this alone. I didn't realize that this new doctor had every intention of doing an amniocentesis that day. I had read enough on the internet to know about the procedure and to know that it carried a risk of miscarriage. I didn't understand why he wanted to do this test, so I challenged him on it. I had already made a firm decision to welcome my child into this world no matter the consequences, because God had given her to me and He had promised never to leave me. I knew it was my awesome responsibility as her mother to give her the utmost care. I was up for the challenge, no matter what. So I proclaimed to this doctor that my mind had been made up, despite the full disclosure that I had been given about what to expect. I told him I refused to have the amniocentesis because of the risk of loss it carried. My daughter had enough challenge facing her already, and I didn't want to add to it. I also told him that we had decided that I'd have a scheduled C-section.

His response shocked me to my core. It really tested my resolve to be ten feet tall and bulletproof throughout her lifetime of adversity. His tactless bedside manner was unbelievable as he casually told me it wouldn't matter which method I chose for delivery, because my daughter would more or less be a vegetable. Yet again, I faced a doctor who offered no hope, and, even worse, he didn't even offer one of those sympathetic, somber frowns. It was as if my child was as disposable as the tissue I was blowing my nose with.

An enormous lump formed in my throat, nearly choking me. I fought back tears and wished I had let my family come with me. But my pride wouldn't allow the waterworks to flow in front of this horrid man. Instead, my natural-born sinner tendency wanted to stab him, and I knew my motherly instincts had already formed as I got a first taste of the momma grizzly bear roaring within me.

I left his office and robotically scurried through mazes of brightly blurred tunnels booming with white noise as I attempted to process how a man like that was ever allowed to work with mothers and infants. I tried to be as invisible as possible and exit the hospital as fast as I could. Once I made it to my vehicle, I let the walls down. I bawled my eyes out. My heart ached for my daughter and the monumental hurdles she would have to overcome.

Around this time, I felt God's presence defending me against the attacks of doubt and fear. He gave me an inexplicable peace, something I had never really felt before. Because of my long history of self-reliance, I had never willingly come to the point where I wanted to rely on God for anything. But this was different. I knew I needed to lean on Him, because peace was not something I could manufacture on my own.

God reminded me of another promise from His Word.

> "Be anxious for nothing, but in everything by prayer
> and supplication, with thanksgiving, let your requests be
> known to God; and the peace of God, which surpasses all
> understanding, will guard your hearts and minds through
> Christ Jesus." Philippians 4:6–7

Because the situation was far beyond my control, I brought everything about my daughter to God in prayer. She has been one of the few things in my life I've been able to release to the Lord successfully.

I am reminded of another woman who released her child to the Lord: Hannah, in the Old Testament. Her son was Samuel. Although hers was a very different set of circumstances from my own, the common thread is that Hannah had also longed for a child. She had been barren and, in those days, if a woman wasn't able to bear children for her husband, she was ridiculed and mocked. Although God tells us through His Word that He closed her womb, we know that she had become bitter from years of childlessness. Hannah, feeling helpless and finding herself in a pit of despair, went to the temple and sought the Lord.

> "She, greatly distressed, prayed to the Lord and wept
> bitterly. She made a vow and said, 'O Lord of hosts, if You
> will indeed look on the affliction of Your maidservant and
> remember me, and not forget Your maidservant, but will
> give Your maidservant a son, then I will give him to the
> Lord all the days of his life...'" 1 Samuel 1:10–11

Hannah sincerely poured her heart out to the Lord, and, in a moment of incredible grace, He remembered her and reopened her womb.

> "It came about in due time, after Hannah had conceived,
> that she gave birth to a son; and she named him Samuel,
> saying 'Because I have asked him of the Lord.'"
> 1 Samuel 1:20

Hannah knew what she prayed for. She was specific. And there was no doubt in her mind that the Lord heard her and answered. In response to His graciousness, she made a promise.

> "For this boy I prayed, and the Lord has given me my
> petition which I asked of Him. So I have also dedicated
> him to the Lord; as long as he lives he is dedicated to the
> Lord." 1 Samuel 1:27–28

There was only one response I could make with my child: dedicate her to the Lord. There was also no doubt in my mind that God was actively working in my life and that He demanded my attention.

Here's what I learned from Hannah's situation:

1. God is in absolute control. He closed Hannah's womb for a period of time. And He reopened it as well.

2. God sees us in our affliction.

3. God's timing is different from ours.

4. God did not forget Hannah.

5. The proper response to God's mercy and blessing in our time of need is to give God full praise and devotion.

After God gave Hannah a son, she prayed with thanksgiving and said that the weak are surrounded with strength, and that strength came directly from the Lord. That is exactly where I found myself, weak apart from God. I knew that my daughter's lifetime of struggles was only beginning, and I needed strength. Like Hannah, I prayed and gave my child back to God. I told Him this was His child and He would have to care for her. I confessed that I was grateful to be her mother for as long as He allowed me to have her.

The Big Day

My C-section was scheduled about ten days before my daughter's actual due date, to ensure that she didn't surprise us and come early. The appointed time to meet my little blessing face to face had finally come. We arrived at the hospital well before the sun revealed itself. Other than being nervous, I was in no pain and couldn't tell you what a contraction was if one had slapped me in the face. For that I was thankful. That was a plus. But the negative was that I was in no pain. So going to get an epidural presented an enormous challenge for me.

I have already shared what it was like for me blindly to take a needle in the back, but I must add that all that trauma was inflicted for nothing. My epidural didn't work.

The moment the needle shot into my spinal cord, my leg jerked and a sharp pain shot through me. But, hey, I had never done this before, so who was I to know what it was supposed to look and feel like? I just went with the flow, silently and timidly following their every instruction.

Once I was on the operating table, just moments before the surgery began, they began sterilizing and scrubbing my big, fat belly. I looked up at the anesthesiologist who was hovering over my face and I told him I could feel that. It felt like sandpaper scrubbing my skin raw. Doctors must like to hear themselves talk, because they make horrible listeners. Much like the doctors who dismissed my comment about my daughter moving in my womb, this one dismissed my observation that I could feel what they were doing as if my most basic sense to feel were a highly scientific phenomenon that I would know nothing about.

Then came the scalpel. I kept coaching myself silently not to be a weenie, because the doctors knew what they were doing and I was just being a wimp. When they sliced into my skin, I squealed like a piglet, though I tried to stifle it. I told the anesthesiologist again that I could feel it. He might as well have rolled his eyes, because he clearly didn't believe me. He told me that I would feel a numb tugging, like at the dentist's office. I thought to myself, "I'd shoot that dentist if he ever put me through that kind of pain." Then the anesthesiologist told me to wiggle my foot. I did. Judging from the look on his face, I wasn't supposed to be able to do that.

Whatever he pumped into my veins at that point erased the rest of the experience. But it only takes a minute to cut a baby out and sew a mom back up, so I had already endured the worst of it. I vaguely remember them doing a tool count so I didn't go home with any extra hardware in my insides, and I remember them stitching me up while I thanked God that it was about to be over.

My daughter's slimy little tail was lifted up, and she didn't make a peep. She was content to be in this new world and didn't fuss about it, but her father was concerned that something was wrong. He asked the doctor why she wasn't crying, and they replied, "Well, do you *want* her to?" They tapped her little behind and she let out the most precious squawk I had ever heard. Just that one little squawk and then she went back to being content.

A team of nurses and doctors had been on standby, waiting for this moment to gently dress the sack that protruded from the opening in my daughter's spine and cover all the exposed nerve endings attached to her spinal cord with a sterile saline wrap. Again, I was so thankful to know of her defect in advance so that I could arrange to have the best care for her the moment she entered this world.

Once they had her cleaned and wrapped, a nurse held her before me. For a brief moment, I was able to see the face of the daughter I loved so deeply. I wasn't given the opportunity to touch or hold her because I was still lying on the operating table being stitched up.

The team in charge of her care immediately took her to an ambulance, and she was transported to the children's hospital where another team of doctors was on standby. One of those doctors was my new hero, the neurosurgeon, who was ready to close the opening in her spine upon arrival.

I don't remember leaving the operating room and getting to a private room, but I do remember being in agony and being unable to go with my daughter to the ambulance to see her off because I began hemorrhaging and was put to bed with doses of morphine and who knows what else. It was a surreal feeling. I knew that I had just had a baby, but she wasn't with me. For three days I lay in the hospital feeling hacked to pieces. It was my own private horror movie, because every breath and blink of the eye was painfully felt in slow motion. Every part of my body seemed to be attached to my abdomen. Going to the restroom was a major ordeal, and I'm pretty sure I begged them to leave a catheter in me, because it took about thirty minutes to shuffle to the toilet, even though it was only a few feet away, and I had no idea how to empty my bladder once I got there, because I could not bend without excruciating pain.

I was thankful for the morphine to help numb the pain, but I felt really weird and started seeing floating, pink, fuzzy elephants, like Dumbo did while he was intoxicated. I also had a reaction that left me clawing at my itchy skin like a paranoid schizophrenic. They gave me something to counteract the symptoms, and I slept a good bit —

as best as I could with big, burly nurses coming in every few hours to massage my fundus, whatever that is, that lay directly beneath my incision, in order to get it to retract to whatever size it was supposed to be. Every couple of hours there was another intrusion, as they attached me to a breast pump for the purpose of convincing my body that I'd had the baby and was ready to nurse. Apparently my body didn't know it needed to do that after a C-section, so the continual act of pumping was supposed to cause milk production.

I wanted to nurse, but the whole mechanical process wearied me. Having to sit up and move any part of my body was enough to make me want to quit, but one of my best friends stayed with me faithfully, and she made sure I didn't. I loved her for her persistence and for knowing that deep down I really didn't want to quit. She stayed with me day and night, and I began to refer to her as the Pump Nazi every time she made me hook up to the machine. She even rubbed my fat, swollen feet, something I am sure few people in this world would have offered to do, and she held my hand in the wee hours of the night when the Viking-sized nurse came in to manhandle my fundus. For that, I am eternally grateful to her.

Eventually the milk came, and the drugs cleared my system. Wonderful friends visited me and honored my no-laugh-zone declaration, because laughing hurt — and that wasn't funny.

My momma has always been my biggest cheerleader, and she loyally stayed by my side, waiting on me hand and foot and bringing me pictures of my little one until I was discharged and was able to go see her wonderfulness for myself. Since my incredible mother hardly left my side, she was there to snap a picture of the moment when I saw my daughter for the first time since delivery. It's a sweet image of our reunion, and it captured how my eyes feasted on her in amazement as I quickly memorized each of her little features.

I couldn't hold my baby until she was about a week old because she had already had her surgery and was belly down in an incubator. She was sunning herself in the warm glow of the light that kept her toasty and comfortable, and she lay there with a grin. It looked like a railroad track crossed her torso from where the neurosurgeon and plastic surgeon teamed up to reassemble her backside and stitch her together.

It was a long week, but we were finally able to take our daughter home and begin watching her grow. We had a list of things to watch for post-surgery, but the biggest concern was keeping an eye on her hydrocephalus. We were instructed to make sure her fontanel, the soft spot on her head, stayed soft. Any firmness or protrusion could indicate too much pressure, and too much pressure would require another operation to place a shunt in her brain. We were told that vomiting and sleepiness were another indication that the pressures were too great. Well, she was a baby who liked to sleep and had severe reflux. So it was very difficult to tell what was serious and what was not, and we spent many nights in the ER going through a series of CAT scans and x-rays, waiting for the on-call neurosurgeon to read the results and determine if we had a serious issue.

About a month later, the decision was made to go ahead and place the shunt in her brain so the cerebrospinal fluid could drain properly. We were aware that there was a good chance it could malfunction and we would be back for more surgery, and that is exactly what we experienced. The first shunt worked for only a couple of weeks before requiring another surgery, called a shunt revision. Several more would follow.

Our daughter had five surgeries in her first year, and I was thankful for the insurance that covered most of it, and for our state's Medicaid program that covered the rest because of her disability. The Medicaid was an answered prayer by itself because, after seeing the doctors' bills, I began to worry about our insurance company's lifetime maximum for her — and this was only year one.

Without question, our daughter was a miracle and a blessing, and she became a continual reminder of God's intervention in my life. I knew that God was incapable of lying and would follow through with the promises in His Word. Here are some rich truths on which He delivered.

1. God fashioned my daughter exactly how He wanted her. She was wonderful, even if most of her doctors couldn't appreciate that fact.

   "For You formed my inward parts; You covered me in my mother's womb. I will praise You, for I am fearfully and wonderfully made; Marvelous are Your works, and that my soul knows very well." Psalm 139:13–14

2. She was a gift He gave to me.

   "Behold, children are a heritage from the Lord, the fruit of the womb is a reward." Psalm 127:3

3. He told me not to be afraid, because He would be there to help me.

   "Thus says the Lord who made you and formed you from the womb, who will help you, do not fear..." Isaiah 44:2

Would the road ahead be easy? Of course not. Did I go into this with eyes wide open and with full disclosure of how rough it would be caring for a child with special needs? Yes, I did. What was it like releasing her, and all the strings of worry, to the Lord? It was like taking in a breath of fresh air and simultaneously exhaling a polluted one that would poison me. It was a miracle, another gift from God, and, through the power of the Holy Spirit, I was given contentment and peace about her and her situation.

CHAPTER 5:

TOOLS FOR DISCOVERY & DISCUSSION

1. In what situations have you been overly anxious and longed for the peace of God?

2. Can you recall a time when you knew God saw you in your affliction? If so, how did you know?

3. How do you feel about children being born with disabilities even though God tells us He is the one who fashions us in the womb and we are wonderfully made? Does this challenge your belief that He is a loving God?

4. Do you believe God when He promises to help you and tells you not to fear?

CHAPTER 5: A SEARCH FOR BIBLICAL TRUTH

TEARS, DISABILITIES, & THE PEACE OF GOD

In chapter 1 we made the correlation between guarding our souls and keeping God's commandments by use of the same Hebrew word in Scripture. This same word appears in Philippians 4:7. We are able to receive the peace of God in order to guard our hearts and minds through whom? We are not given the monumental task of keeping and honoring God's word (and our composure) without the help of Jesus! His assistance is never more evident than during our trials.

God's peace and grace is lavishly bestowed upon us, particularly when overwhelmed with affliction. Are we alone in our struggles? Absolutely not! Read 2 Kings 20:5. God sees our tears. What does He do with them? Read Psalm 56:8. Our tears are not only noticed by God, but they are valued. Isaiah and John both record prophesies for us to savor regarding our tears. Read Isaiah 25:8-9 and Revelation 21:4 and describe the hope that we have as believers in Christ.

We cling to hope during our journey on this earth. Trials come and they go. Caring for special-needs children can certainly be a trial some endure for many years, but as King Solomon learned, we must have a proper perspective and keep our eyes fixed on Jesus. We are told in 2 Corinthians 4:16-18 to not to lose heart. Why? In John 9:1-3, why did Jesus say the blind man was given a disability? As Christians, we must grasp the bigger picture and always hold onto the foundational building blocks of our faith. Why are we created (Isaiah 43:7)? In whose image are we created

(Genesis 1:26-27)? We are all created for His glory. Perhaps you or someone you love has a disability. Don't lose heart. God doesn't make mistakes. He will give you peace that surpasses all understanding (Philippians 4:7) and strength to endure your storm.

CHAPTER 6

Same Song, Second Verse

I had gotten a taste of divine contentment and not only did it prove to be lasting and steadfast in those days, but it continues to sustain me. To this day I don't worry about the challenges faced by my daughter. We face them and move on. She continues to be in the Lord's hands.

But the contentment I felt with her disability didn't project into other areas of my life, because I never released other areas of my life to God. I was still chained to the snares of pride, greed, and self-sufficiency. I was still searching for my laughing place, and the more I chased material satisfaction, the more I got scratched by thorny situations. I was bound, restless, and struggling to carry on.

We had wanted to sell our little starter home several years before my daughter was born, but I was too cheap to pay a real estate agent. So the for-sale-by-owner sign went in the yard and stayed there for what felt like an eternity. The problem with selling the house was that our subdivision had multiple phases and hundreds of houses. We purchased in the initial phase of development, so the lure of buying a brand-new home versus a used one was difficult to compete with. In addition, the market was saturated and there were sellers just like us on every corner. The brand new homes had builder incentives and first-time buyer programs, and their list price was essentially what we owed on our home. Remember, I failed to negotiate a better purchase price when I bought the house, so we probably owed far more on our house than everybody else owed on theirs. We couldn't afford to pay an agent; we would lose money. To top it off, our little home had only two bedrooms and did not have a garage — two more strikes against us. Worse, our "for sale" sign went in the yard immediately before the horrific events of 9/11. Who could have predicted that terrorists would infiltrate our defense system, shake our country to the core, and devastate our economic markets? It certainly wasn't something I foresaw, but it became a reality we dealt with as the red sign in our yard began to fade in the sun.

I had prayed for patience as we waited for a buyer. Yes, the "P word" actually did come from my lips, and after more than a decade of trials since that simple prayer for patience, I have jokingly regretted ever muttering it. Patience is *not* a virtue — at least, it's not one of mine. For some reason, God chose not to dispense it when He fashioned me, and I'm sure He chuckled a great deal knowing the childish behavior its absence would evoke.

No, God didn't hand patience to me on a silver platter as I had hoped; rather, it's been something produced over time and through a variety of situations.

We pulled the sign from the yard just prior to our daughter's birth, knowing that she was where our focus needed to be. When I prayed for patience, I wanted it to address my antsiness in selling the house, but God took it to a whole other level. After my daughter was born, I was confronted by a series of questions I didn't have answers to, and I wouldn't for quite some time.

Would she ever talk?

Would she ever walk?

Would she have to be in a wheelchair?

Would she have to wear leg braces?

Would she have to be catheterized?

Would she ever get out of diapers?

Would she ever outgrow the need for a shunt?

My questions kept coming, and her specialists continually answered that we would just have to wait and see. Only time would tell. Even though I was at peace with her condition, the not knowing sometimes irritated me. It tested my patience, or my lack of it.

A few verses that were popular in church caused me some real struggles because I failed to follow them fully. These were hard truths to begin with, but even more so for a believer who still required milk instead of meat for spiritual nourishment.

> "My brethren, count it all joy when you fall into various trials, knowing that the testing of your faith produces patience. But let patience have its perfect work, that you may be perfect and complete, lacking nothing."
> James 1:2–4

My study of God's Word didn't have much depth because I was not a seasoned student and had never taken the time to become one. I didn't consider context or look closely at every word; rather, I glossed over them as I read speedily through the day's passages. So I missed a few things. A lot of things.

Many people would be baffled by the idea of being joyful in trials. That's not an easy thing to grasp, but since I had already tasted God's joy and peace with my daughter's situation, I was okay with that part. I believed that my trials would produce patience, so I found steadfast strength in *knowing* that it would come. I just didn't know when it would come, what it would look like, and how to handle it once I got it.

One little word in that verse, *let*, has major implications. If we overlook these three little letters, we could easily overlook our responsibility to *allow* God to work in our lives and to *allow* the problem we are facing to be used as a catalyst in building our character while not being overwhelmed; ultimately, we can miss a blessing.

I'm queen of holding onto things, of not letting go, but I've discovered that if I don't release a problem to God and allow Him to work in my life, then I cannot expect to obtain His peace and patience and let Him mature me into the person He wants me to be. God is fully capable of transforming us into whatever He wants us to be through His omnipotence, but He has chosen to give us a choice instead. God most desires a loving and genuine relationship from us. If He willfully forced us to love Him as if we were puppets on a string, then the relationship wouldn't be real. C.S. Lewis writes about how God forgoes His power with regard to our choices in *The Screwtape Letters*,

> *You must have often wondered why [God] does not make more use of His power to be sensibly present to human souls in any degree He chooses and at any moment. But you now see that the Irresistible and the Indisputable are the two weapons which the very nature of His scheme forbids Him to use. Merely to override a human will (as His felt presence in any but the faintest and most mitigated degree would certainly do) would be for Him useless. He cannot ravish. He can only woo.*

As for me, the choices I had been making weren't allowing Him access to all areas of my life, and as a result, I constantly felt like something was lacking.

So the "for sale" sign went back in the yard and I went back to chasing the dream of a bigger house and better stuff. The house still didn't sell, and I couldn't understand why my prayer wasn't being answered, why my house sat dormant on the market, with absolutely no interest from anyone.

"You ask and you do not receive, because you ask amiss, that you may spend it on your pleasures." James 4:3

It wasn't inherently wrong to have nice things, because God likes to give good gifts to His children. But it became wrong for *me*, because I began to idolize fancy things; obtaining them consumed me. Like most addicts, I didn't realize the effect that my obsession was having on me or anyone else around me. But God did. My infatuations violated one of His most basic commandments, and to give me everything I wanted would not be in my best interest.

As parents, what do we do when our child steps out of line? We discipline them. Likewise, God began disciplining me as He drew me nearer and asked me to rely upon Him alone. But just as any spoiled child will throw a tantrum when denied the candy at the checkout line, I persisted in my self-reliance, stubbornly pursuing a better job, a better title, and a better home.

After my daughter was born, I returned to my career, but I worked only four days a week because the number of doctors' appointments and surgeries made it extremely difficult to hold down a full-time job. The firm I worked for was wonderful in being flexible and sympathetic towards my needs as a mother, and having the extra day off made all the difference in the world for scheduling my daughter's care without missing more work. The four-day work schedule worked for a while, but after a year of auditing smaller clients that weren't too challenging, I noticed that the younger crop of new hires was advancing up the ladder, and I wasn't. They were taking more challenging engagements which provided better opportunities for them to show off their skills, and with the recognitions of their skills came promotions —and raises. I was envious of the new hires, whom I meticulously took time to train. Especially since that kind of training wasn't available when I started with the firm, and I was the one who had created the training program after realizing the need for it. I was happy for their achievements and proud that they were doing well, but I was also discouraged that I seemed to be sitting idly, going nowhere.

I was still snared by my ambition, and it dawned on me that I wouldn't be getting another title at the pace I was going. Through an unexpected conversation, I learned that my annual cost of living adjustments had been surpassed by the newcomers' promotions. Apparently signing bonuses and starting salaries had been increased significantly to lure more recruits, so it didn't take a whole lot for there to be a flat pay scale. But I wasn't okay with that. I had five years of experience on these youngsters, and I reasoned that there should be a noticeable difference in our compensation. It was the straw that broke the camel's back. I had been patiently paying my dues and waiting for a door of opportunity to open, because I felt that going into private industry would work better and have more meaning for me. I got tired of working with historical data. Our clients didn't seem to want auditors on their premises, and I had a yearning to be somewhere I was appreciated, somewhere I could make a difference. I wanted to have purpose and belong to something bigger.

On the same day that unexpected conversation revealed more than I wanted to know, I received a phone call from an accounting recruitment company. We called them headhunters, and we frequently received calls from them on our personal phones as they tried to shift talent from one company to another by dangling dollars and more lucrative positions. I was conditioned to respond sharply and rudely, because these headhunters were notorious for not taking "no" for an answer, so I flatly replied, "I want to have my cake and to eat it, too, and if you can't give me a job with better hours and better pay then don't call me back."

I thought he wouldn't call back, and, as I sat there stewing on what I'd learned about my current employment, I lost my motivation to work. But, at the end of the day, that headhunter called again. He told me of a position and said that he couldn't reveal the company, but the management wanted to interview me, knowing I would be asking for a flexible schedule and more money. Was he kidding me?

This sort of thing never fell into my lap! I agreed to interview just days later, on my Friday off, because I could easily make the appointment without tipping off the firm. It worked out perfectly. When the headhunter gave me the details of the interview he had arranged and finally disclosed the company involved, I was shocked. It was a large, well-known non-profit, and the controller interviewing me was an old friend who had worked with me at my current firm years before. She was excited that I was interviewing and gave me the Assistant Controller position on the spot.

I was elated. Earlier in the week I had reached the pinnacle of frustration, and by the end of the week I had a new job. Even better, the new job didn't involve recording billable hours and working during tax season. Yes, I was given my piece of cake and I got to eat it, too. There was one small drawback: of all my auditing clients at the firm, I hated non-profits the most. The accounting was different, and I was much more comfortable working with manufacturing and for-profit clients. But I didn't care. The door of opportunity had opened, and I was eager to walk through.

My new position had a corporate feel, and this non-profit wasn't hurting for money, holding desks together with duct tape, using smoke signals to communicate, or behaving in any of the other poverty-driven ways I'd seen at other non-profit clients around town. In fact, my position came with its very own office, a fantastic window, and a door. The new company had about the same number of employees as the firm, but with a much more diverse set of personalities. Each department had its own hierarchy, and it was only a matter of time before my boss was promoted and I was asked to take on her position, along with that coveted new title. It was still like climbing the corporate ladder, but there were fewer rungs at this place.

The vice-president of our finance department was a sweet old man, and he showed me preferential treatment. Somehow I became his favorite employee, and my friend and I joked about it often — behind closed doors, of course. He was good to me, particularly when I needed help raising funds to send my daughter to a special school in another state, a school that would help her with her physical disability. He allowed donations to come through the entity's tax-exempt structure so that donors who supported our cause could claim a tax deduction for their gifts.

Evaluations were vastly different from those at the firm, and getting lucrative raises in addition to having rare benefits and company-paid luxury travel pleased me. I took advantage of the vice-president's preferential treatment and was easily able to talk him into higher raises. He didn't care. As long as I kept doing the work and making improvements to their antiquated ways, it was less work that he would have to do, and it afforded him more time to sit in his office surfing the internet or wander through the halls socializing. We made his department look good, which ultimately led to generous raises and bonuses for him, too. I was thankful he was willing to share the wealth.

During this time, our little house finally sold, and I was able to move forward with building the dream home. My friends at the old firm who were driven in the same ways as me advised us to build the biggest house we could afford with our current paycheck because more raises would come. So far that had been true. This dream home kept me awake at night as plans and details spun in my head. It kept me distracted at work, as I searched the internet and polished those ideas that filled my mind. After living in the starter home for five years, I knew exactly which improvements I longed for in the dream home, I had the entire thing built, decorated, and landscaped in my head before we ever purchased the set of plans.

Still chasing the title.

Still chasing the American Dream.

Still wanting more.

By all appearances I was living the American Dream, and it felt like everything was clicking in my material world — except I *wasn't* living a dream. Once the new dream home was built, I had the same issues. My belongings didn't talk to me; bigger bills landed in our mailbox; there was a larger property to take care of, and now I had a daughter with special needs. Much of this responsibility was left for me to handle. My spouse's absence became more prominent as I nagged about financial concerns and needing help around the house. The more I attempted to control, the more I was given to take control of. It was a frustrating cycle.

I preferred doing things my way, and because I was pursuing perfection, "my way" came with very high expectations. Pride whispered to me that my way was the best way. Even when help was offered, the tasks weren't done to my satisfaction and I let it be known. I still carried that snare of pride, and it was slowly killing my relationship. The enemy, the great trapper, surely sneered at the hole I was digging for myself.

Loneliness, weariness, and frustration caused my words to become sharp.

Oh, the power we have in our words.

When used carefully, they build up. They encourage. They tattoo smiles across our faces and put sparkles in our eyes. They cause our hearts to flutter. They charm us. They make us feel royal. Special. They affirm what needs to be said. They give security and squash the enemy's lies. They are like medicine for the soul. The thought of them can make us bubble up in joyful laughter. Days, months, or even years after we've received them. They give us new perspective. Fresh meaning. Continued hope. They offer promises we hold on to.

When used poorly, they tear down. They devalue. They dangle past failures before us. They tell us we'll never be good enough. They can deceitfully hide what lies beneath. Or they can expose it. They can leave us bewildered all night long as they echo through our head. They fan the flames of insecurity. They crush the spirit. They cut deep, creating wounds no man can heal. They leave scars, scars that may appear to be healed on the surface, but that can still be felt deep within. They disappoint. They confirm our worst fears. They can scare us to death.

I've heard it said that for every negative word spoken, at least three or four positive ones are needed to repair the damage. I'd argue that it takes a whole lot more than that, or at least for me it does. You see, the thing with words is they can't be taken back. Once they're out there, there's no retrieving them. There's no convenient "undo" button to click.

We hope our words are on target, but what if it is a miss and the destruction is far more devastating than ever imagined? Should we have actually pulled the trigger or waited? In the end, was it worth it to say what we most *wanted*, not necessarily *needed*, to say in the heat of the moment? We filter our water, so why don't we filter our words? Why do we speak with reckless abandon? Why do we spend more time picking out our clothes in the morning than we do carefully selecting our words — one of the things that has the greatest potential to build up or tear down a relationship?

As I think back over my journey, it's much easier to see now what transpired then. I was bitter in my marriage, but, ironically, I was growing closer to the Lord. And as much as I pursued a deeper relationship with the Lord, so did the enemy fervently pursue me by placing blind spots in my path. Blind spots which prevented me from seeing the truth of how hypocritical I was being.

> "Does a spring send forth fresh water and bitter from the
> same opening? James 3:11

I had disgruntled thoughts and was like a fierce badger at home as I let those thoughts turn into unfiltered words. But in public and at church, I masked the troubles I faced in my personal life. I was able to talk the talk. By then, I could quote Scripture and was quite familiar with its precepts. Unfortunately, I didn't let all the verses I memorized do their work and change me. I didn't allow these truths to fully sink in. I was in an oppressive blind spot.

> "Who is wise and understanding among you? Let him show
> by good conduct that his works are done in meekness of
> wisdom. But if you have bitter envy and self-seeking in your
> hearts, do not boast and lie against the truth. This wisdom

does not descend from above, but is earthly, sensual, demonic. For where envy and self-seeking exist, confusion and every evil thing are there. But the wisdom that is from above is first pure, then peaceable, gentle, willing to yield, full of mercy and good fruits, without partiality and without hypocrisy. Now the fruit of righteousness is sown in peace by those who make peace." James 3:13–18

I wasn't displaying Godly wisdom, and I certainly wasn't meek or gentle in my actions and responses. I was bitter as a result of my own selfish seeking of worldly things, and I was confused as to why they didn't provide lasting satisfaction. I had bought into a lie as I chased everything under the sun. My life didn't show the fruits of righteousness. I didn't allow Godly wisdom to speak truth into my life. I had no peace. I wasn't willing to yield to anyone or anything if it contradicted my way. I was not merciful. I was a big, fat hypocrite. I was snared.

It was the same ol' song, second verse.

CHAPTER 6:

TOOLS FOR DISCOVERY & DISCUSSION

1. Do you believe that God is in absolute control? How do you feel about His giving us a choice to pursue Him?

2. Have you ever prayed for something and it never seemed to be answered? Why do you think this is so? Have you considered looking closely to see if your request aligns with God's will and if it is in your best interest?

3. What are your thoughts on the power of words? Describe how you've been impacted by words you've received or words you've spoken. Have you found it difficult to forgive harsh words spoken?

4. Have you ever considered yourself snared in an oppressive blind spot such as hypocrisy? What role does the enemy play in keeping us blind to our shortcomings?

CHAPTER 6: A SEARCH FOR BIBLICAL TRUTH

OUR WORDS DO MATTER

Read Ephesians 4:29-32. What does verse 30 tell us that our
corrupt words do to the Holy Spirit of God? Did you know that
our words and actions are indicators of what is going on in our
hearts? Read Matthew 12:33-37 paying close attention to what
Jesus says in verse 36. Can we imagine what that day may look
like?

In the last chapter we talked about being created in the image of
God. Our minds, the center for our bodies' intelligent thoughts
and emotional feelings are fashioned in the likeness of God. One
way Satan, the enemy of our souls, is most effective in blinding us
to our sin is by manipulating our thoughts. What concern did Paul
have for the Corinthians in 2 Corinthians 11:3? He was concerned
that they would be deceived just as Eve had been in the Garden of
Eden. The lies we believe affect our words and actions. Allowing
a loose tongue and coarse speech into our lives is a slippery slope.
It can get out of hand before we even realize it! Philippians 4:8 is
a great filter to use for our thoughts and desires. If our thoughts
and desires do not pass this litmus test, they should be rejected.
Undesirable thoughts should only be verbalized with a heart of
confession and repentance in prayer or with another believer who
can assist us with the struggle (James 5:16).

CHAPTER 7

A Fantastic Pharisee

Solomon stated that whoever guards his soul would be far from thorns and snares. I hadn't guarded my heart and soul; a thorn of marital discord had become firmly embedded, and it became more and more infected over time.

I had discovered that my faith was going to carry me through the storms of life, so I attended church every time the doors were open. I longed to be there. God was really doing a transforming work in me, but, by the time I began surrendering to His will, my marriage was in such a mess that I didn't have any clue how to fix it. There were so many layers of offense that we could hardly speak to each other without the putrid reek of disdain dripping from our words. We were living two separate lives under the same roof; our paths seldom crossed, and we almost never occupied the same space at the same time.

I still didn't give up, though. When we first married I wasn't walking in Christian faith, but what God had begun revealing to me was amazing and, in light of my recent growing faith, I made it my mission to change my man. I knew how wonderfully God was changing me, and I longed for him to be more fascinated with spiritual things too. I took every opportunity to preach at him with the hopes of a positive outcome, but I could never understand why he wasn't receptive to my pointed sermons.

I would have made a fantastic Pharisee. They were quick to point out others' flaws too. In Jesus' day, this Jewish religious sect was concerned with keeping the Old Testament law, so much so that they added much more to the law's requirements through custom and tradition. Poof! They made religion a checklist of do's and don'ts.

The very reason God sent Jesus was to abolish the law. By living it perfectly, by fulfilling every single prophecy in the Old Testament, and, ultimately, by being the perfect sacrifice, Jesus abolished the law's system of do's and don'ts. The purpose of the death, burial, and resurrection of Jesus was to institute a new covenant of grace with us. Through our faith in Jesus's work, we are saved. Our creator has longed for us to have a personal relationship with Him since he placed mankind in the Garden of Eden, but the Pharisees couldn't see that. They were too busy checking off their lists and, in doing so, pointing out everyone else's shortcomings.

We know how Jesus felt about the Pharisees because He spoke directly about their behavior and traditions. Right off the bat, Jesus addressed their hypocrisy.

> "Then Jesus spoke to the multitudes and to His disciples, saying, 'The scribes and Pharisees sit in Moses' seat.
> Therefore whatever they tell you to observe, that observe

and do, but do not do according to their works; for they say, and do not do." Matthew 23:1–3

Jesus didn't condemn the law or the teaching and following of it, but He condemned the disparity that the Pharisees showed in their daily actions when compared to the mechanical compliance they taught. They were blind to the areas where they fell short. Spiritually blind to their hypocrisy. They weren't keeping the law fully, as they expected of everyone else.

Jesus continued to expose the Pharisees and condemned their unrealistic expectations.

> "'For they bind heavy burdens, hard to bear, and lay them on men's shoulders; but they themselves will not move them with one of their fingers.'" Matthew 23:4

Only Jesus lived a perfect life. But the Pharisees projected their expectations of perfection onto others and placed a burden on the people that couldn't be carried. These burdensome rules were created by man, not by the Lord.

I've been in the same trap. I've demanded perfection time and time again. I've expected sacrifices to be made, but I wasn't willing to budge or compromise on any points of my own. I wanted loving kindness shown towards me, but my bitterness kept me from showing loving kindness to someone who offended me. I could sulk with the best of them!

In addition to exposing hypocrisy, Jesus addressed the Pharisees' pretension. He pointed out their showy attempts to impress people while He knew what really transpired in their hearts.

> "'Woe to you, scribes and Pharisees, hypocrites! For you devour widows' houses, and for a pretense make long

prayers. Therefore you will receive greater condemnation.'"
Matthew 23:14

Oh, how much time have I wasted trying to make people think more highly of me than they should? Pretension was a mask I wore for a long time. And Jesus used my ol' buddy Cotton to shed some light on my preoccupation with pleasing others and putting on a show.

It was bunko night. Our group consisted of twelve extremely dedicated women who, rain or shine, showed up once a month to roll some dice and talk about life. I relished that time with my friends, and for nearly ten years we had babies together, rejoiced in adoptions, grieved losses of little ones, endured rocky marriages, steamed over petty squabbles, laughed until it hurt, and on and on. We just lived life together. And it was marvelous. My relationships were real, but I was preoccupied with keeping up appearances, especially, in this case, the appearance of my home. I cared what my friends thought about me.

Now any woman caught in this phase knows what I'm talking about. Just the thought of having company required deep cleaning and organization of the remotest closet in the house. It sounds absurd now, but, at the time, I couldn't understand why no man would ever relate to this concept. Why he couldn't understand that all of the bathrooms had to be spotless, for this drove of women would surely meander throughout the house to simply "take a look." Stress. Fear. Anxiety. I loved these women, and they loved me. But I wouldn't be caught dead having a home that wasn't perfect, and I let fear and the notion of being less than perfect dominate my behavior.

It was my turn to host bunko. I spent the entire day scrubbing, straightening, decorating, and displaying, so everything would be *just right*. The one thing I neglected to care for that day was my sweet Cotton. Poor Cotton. He was shuffled into the laundry room and locked away. The other minor detail I failed to tend to was the small waste can in the laundry room that was filled with mounds of elementary school worksheets and art projects whose time had expired on the wall of honor — I mean, the fridge. One of the projects I trashed had something to do with a Mardi Gras celebration; it was covered in purple, green, and gold glitter and glued-on Cheerios.

Well, ol' Cotton got his payback. Can't blame him. After a day of neglect, he had a little snack of Cheerios while I was wrapping up my delightful evening serving a dessert of my own in the other room. It was banana pudding, but this was no ordinary banana pudding; it was a special *Southern Living* recipe that replaced the traditional vanilla wafers with the superior Nutter Butter cookies. And there were other creamy goodies in it besides the box of Jell-O pudding. It was ... special. It was the high point of the evening for me, because I had already sampled it, and it was divine. I just knew everyone else would agree.

Best I can recall, one of the meanderers made her way back to the laundry room to "take a look." She opened the door, and Cotton charged forth into freedom. Having forgotten where he was, and missing the fact that he practically had two legs crossed as he bounced up and down at the front door begging to be let out, it happened. Right there in the living room. One big ol' stinkin' pile of sparkly poo. Yep, it glittered. Just like gold.

Women scattered like it was a bomb scene, and technically, it was. Before anyone could enjoy a bite of my banana pudding extraordinaire, the stampede had made its way out the door; the gagging sounds faded with the thundering crowd. The deed done, Cotton sat over in the corner with a toothy, sparkling grin that brought to mind the "ching" of an Orbit chewing gum commercial. At least that's how it replays in my head.

I hardly recall even getting a good-bye that night as a green cloud permeated the room and bowls of pudding fell to the floor during the exodus, but I know that isn't really true, because we laughed about that night for years. It's been marked as one of the most memorable bunko nights ever. Thanks, Cotton.

That night reminded me of one of my favorite lines from the movie *Steel Magnolias*: "An ounce of pretension is worth a pound of manure." Amen to that. I got what I deserved that bunko night. Technically, I don't think one could call it manure, but it sure was close enough!

The Pharisees were full of manure too, or at least full of themselves, as Jesus pointed out when he confronted their pretentious acts to keep up appearances, while they neglected what truly matters.

> "'Woe to you, scribes and Pharisees, hypocrites! For you cleanse the outside of the cup and dish, but inside they are full of extortion and self-indulgence. Blind Pharisee, first cleanse the inside of the cup and dish, that the outside of them may be clean also.'" Matthew 23:25–26

I had a heart problem. Not the kind you need to visit a cardiologist for, but the kind you need to encounter the Creator for. My self-indulgence had already gotten me into a pickle, pursuing lofty things and standing my ground to protect them, and the pretentious mask I wore to cover it all was exhausting. So regardless of how well I dressed up and pretended that all was well in my life, a dark storm brewed on the inside.

The mouth speaks what is filling the heart, and my frustration and anger spewed out and got me into more trouble. Most of my sharp, bitter arrows were directed to the target at home, my spouse. There came a point when I had to reach out for help from my most trusted counselors. I was dying inside, and the mask was becoming more difficult to wear.

> "'Woe to you, scribes and Pharisees, hypocrites! For you are like whitewashed tombs which indeed appear beautiful

outwardly, but inside are full of dead men's bones and all uncleanness.'" Matthew 23:27

I didn't want anyone to know the real story at home. Not even family. So I confided in a select couple that I knew wouldn't tell me what I *wanted* to hear, but would tell me what I *needed* to hear. I knew that anyone could, and probably would, convince me the best and easiest way was out, and I was so weary I might have been talked into it. But I knew these friends wouldn't do that; they would give me only sound Biblical advice.

They listened to me spew poison and filth more times than I can count. I unloaded. I cried. The bitterness was prominent, and I loathed the situation I was in. My counselors always encouraged me with this assurance, "God's not going to take you out into the desert, flip you a quarter, and tell you to call someone who cares. That's just not how He works." And thank God for that! Because I begged God for grace. For mercy. For His help. For resolution.

It's unfortunate for our culture, but many people find themselves in difficult situations and broken marriages. It's not what God designed for us, but He does allow us to make choices and suffer the consequences. Why, then, do I say that my actions and reactions in this seemingly impossible situation were hypocritical? It would be easy to say that my responses were natural, or even justified. However, I know that I did not give grace or mercy at home. I was judgmental, and I wasn't willing to share with others what had been so freely given to me: grace and forgiveness.

Although I no longer had my old "we're not snobs" t-shirt from college, I still presented myself in a way that said "I'm better than you," and that mindset had been engrained in my life for so long that it felt natural. When I began to allow God back into my life and had a more constant awareness of His presence, I put a religious twist to the same mentality. With that attitude, why would anyone want to hear about God and how He was working in my life? It was a gross misrepresentation of His loving character.

To proclaim the gospel while refusing to address obvious areas of rebellion is a form of hypocrisy, and that's exactly how the Pharisees presented themselves. I would have made a fantastic Pharisee.

CHAPTER 7:

TOOLS FOR DISCOVERY & DISCUSSION

1. Have you ever been hypocritical about something? If so, what?

2. Have you ever tried to impress someone and wore a mask of pretension? Why was it important for you to impress this particular person(s)? Does fear of rejection drive your masquerade?

CHAPTER 7: A SEARCH FOR BIBLICAL TRUTH

HYPOCRISY: WORKS & WORDS

Reading through Matthew 23, we saw that Jesus gave strong warnings to the Pharisees for their hypocrisy. First, we see in verse 3 that their works did not line up with God's Law that they were teaching. What does Paul say in Ephesians 2:8-10 about works? How does one find salvation (verse 8)? The answer is simple. Our faith pleases God (Hebrews 11:6) and because of it, He graciously gives us the gift of salvation. What does NOT save us (verse 9)? Verse 10 tells us we were created to do good works. They are important, because the good works appointed for us will ultimately point others to Him and give Him glory. Now, what does James say about works in James 2:14-26? Paul's point in his letter to the Ephesians was that faith alone is what saves us. James does not contradict Paul's point but rather develops the argument by saying that if one has faith, he will want to do the good works set before him (verse 18). It is the belief and love of God that is the driving force behind the works we do. It is not about working through a merit system to find favor with God in order to earn salvation. Salvation is a gift through faith.

Returning to Matthew 23:3, Jesus not only addressed the Pharisees' works, but He also addressed their words. The analogy in Matthew 23:25 exposes the need to cleanse which part of the cup? With what instrument does the hypocrite destroy his neighbor according to Proverbs 11:9? What contrasts do we see in Proverbs 10:11? Again, we see Jesus focusing on the conditions of our hearts, the wells from which we speak (Matthew 12:34, James 1:26) and act.

CHAPTER 8

Mission to Mexico

Crossing the Border

Opportunity knocked in the midst of my storm as my church assembled a team to go on a mission trip to Mexico. I had never considered going on a foreign mission trip before, but I felt a desperate longing to go on this one. I eagerly signed the forms required to join the team and was asked to raise funds to cover my costs.

My only fundraising experience was the time we needed help to send my daughter to a special school, and even then, I wasn't really involved with the actual fundraising. A couple of driven friends spearheaded the fundraising efforts by selling Boston Butts to half the county, and all I really did was deliver the product. My 4-Runner became the meat paddy wagon, and the smell of smoked pork permeated its interior as I drove those butts to every Tom, Dick, and Harry in the tri-state area. Raising funds was way out of my comfort zone. I didn't like asking people for money; I preferred to be self-sufficient. I was afraid people would think that I was just asking for a handout, that I was not willing to do something for myself. It went against my work ethic. But I did raise *some* of the funds — the easy "asks" to Mom, Dad, Grandma, and Grandpa — and I considered that a valiant effort. Thankfully, an anonymous gift was given to the church on my behalf, and I was able to write a check for the remaining balance.

In all my travels, I had only ventured outside of the U.S. once, and that was a trip to Jamaica before passports were required. The immigration officer accepted a copy of my birth certificate for entrance, but I thought he was going to put me on an immediate return flight home because my married name (obviously) was not reflected on my birth certificate. I had not been told to bring a marriage certificate to show the proper paper trail of my change in identity. A friend who traveled with me was in a worse predicament. Like me, she brought only her birth certificate, but she had been married, divorced, and remarried. He didn't like that either. Our Southern charm did not work on the Jamaican. He demanded, "Why should I let you into my country?" It was hard to take him seriously with his thick, Jamaican accent, but we found out very quickly that he was *not* kidding, and that he held the keys to our entry. It was as if Mary Poppins cracked a whip and scolded us like two little children so we'd stop giggling and step back into line.

In any case, times had changed since the trip to Jamaica. After the tragedy of 9/11, international travel now required passports. Even if one hadn't been required to fly into Mexico, I would have gone through the trouble to acquire a passport anyway, because I decided I didn't want to face another Jamaican-style chiding in a foreign country. Obtaining a passport required advance planning but wasn't much of a challenge. The challenge was the fact that I didn't speak Spanish. I wasn't fond of the high school Spanish teacher, so I opted to take German instead, as if that would ever be a language

I'd use in Mississippi. Two years of German in high school and two semesters in college really did me no good. But I could count to ten in Spanish, and I knew a couple of colors and about five other words. Basics covered, right?

Culture shock began as soon as the trip started. Thankfully, our team leader was fluent in Spanish, because, oddly enough, counting to ten was of no use in going through airport customs. I had the deer-in-the-headlights look. Much to my surprise, I learned that most of the officers knew English, but they only spoke it if they had to. I thought they found satisfaction in my glazed expression as I fumbled in the Spanish-English dictionary, which I found completely useless in conversation. How far would they let me go and how stupid would they let me look before they spit out fluent English?

To further humble me, I was one of the lucky few to get a random bag search — underwear flying everywhere. All the Latinos standing by didn't concern me much; I would never see them again. But I shriveled in humiliation when I locked eyes with the members of my group and a voice whispered in my head, *"I have to go to church with these people."* I've learned that you get to know people quite well on a mission trip as you operate as a cohesive unit through any number of mishaps, even showing your underwear to the world.

Once we arrived at the airport in Monterrey, it felt like we were thrown into the Mexican hat dance as we entered a cab that was, apparently, exempt from any safety precautions. Our driver swerved to and fro through traffic, laid on the horn, and barely missed concrete pillars supporting overhead bypasses and strategically placed in the middle of our road — kind of like the awkward pole dead-center in a Wal-Mart aisle that leaves folks struggling to navigate their carts around the obstacle.

I was relieved to make it to the hotel, which was comfortably modern and felt like any typical hotel I'd stayed at in the States. But the morning breakfast buffet had a strange variety of foods that I wasn't accustomed to. I gravitated to the most familiar dish, scrambled eggs, but the greenish hot dogs lodged in the midst of them discouraged me from scooping a hearty portion onto my plate.

A nervous travel tummy and green weenies caused me to pass on breakfast, as if we would be dropping by a more familiar IHOP later in the morning. I'm sure I presumed that something would conveniently be available at my disposal when my tummy settled and I was ready to eat. Presumptions aren't always correct.

I was strangely caught between two worlds. This modern Mexican city was a weird blend of familiar comforts and labels found at home, but with the language transformed into foreign gibberish. We were clearly *not* at home. There was no IHOP available, and being with a group of people adhering to an itinerary set by our local host revealed to me that *it ain't all about me.* Day one's lesson: food — get it while it's hot, and get it while you can.

Pure Worship

After leaving the hotel one Sunday morning, we visited a little community church that impressed me. The small, cinder block building operated as a facility to tutor children and serve meals to hundreds of people throughout the week and transformed back into a worship center on Sunday. Depending on the capacity in which the building was being used, chairs and podiums were easily placed, configured, and removed as needed. It was plain. No carpet. No décor. But as volunteers took their places with their instruments on the makeshift podium, the place came alive. With our white skin and American mannerisms, we stuck out, but we were given a warm welcome and a place of honor on the front row as they patiently translated the entire service for our benefit.

It was amazing.

The songs were familiar, though they were sung in another language. Anyone who knows me knows that I can't recite the lyrics to a single song in this world. It's just not my gift. I've botched more songs and been laughed at more times than I can count because my version of what the artist said was ridiculously different than the actual lyrics. So when I recognized the worship and praise songs, I kicked myself for being horrible with lyrics as I racked my hollow brain for the translated version. It wasn't there. I glared at the words conveniently printed in Spanish on the overhead screen, but they were foreign. And I kicked myself again for never foreseeing that I'd ever visit our neighboring country and that "Sprechen Sie Deutsch?" would be of no use once I got there. (I still haven't been to Germany, and the once-learned but unused language has faded from memory.) My only recourse was to do my best to recite the words, in Spanish, and I was thankful that the church members sang loud enough that they'd never know I had butchered yet another song.

Aside from my idiosyncrasies, the service was an incredible experience. I had never worshiped like I did that morning in Mexico. The Holy Spirit transcended my limitations and somehow I knew exactly what they were singing. This part of the worship service was all in Spanish, because trying to interpret a song line by line would just be weird. It was unbridled worship. I had never before been in a congregation where there wasn't someone who was distracted, or apathetically taking a nap, or acutely aware of the people sitting around and afraid to lift hands of praise in fear of being thought of as *spiritually kooky*. No, this was nothing like our American churches — or at least the handful of denominations I had ever visited. It was pure worship. Full participation. And it was the most refreshing thing I could have experienced at that time in my spiritual journey.

The openness of the testimonies shared thoroughly convicted me and was a stark contrast to the masquerade that I, and probably everyone else I knew in church, presented. It chipped away at the barrier guarding my heart when certain women stood and shared their stories.

One woman praised God for answering her prayer, a simple prayer about being able to buy a small plastic slide for her toddler's birthday. God miraculously provided the funds that she didn't have, and she was deeply grateful that she could purchase the gift. I had never prayed like that. I never felt the need to rely on God for the little things, because I was so self-sufficient. I had never struggled with going to the store and wondering if I would be able to afford a birthday present for my child. I felt so ashamed of my ungratefulness. I was humbled by her sincerity and gratitude for things I had overlooked and considered mundane. Her simple story, tearfully shared, stuck with me.

The worship was uninhibited. There was no scheduled time frame or good Baptists checking their watches so that they could screech out of the parking lot at noon in order to beat the Methodists to the local steakhouse for lunch. In Mexico, lunchtime came and went as the worship service ran its course, and, by the time we were done and said our good-byes, I realized that I wished I had scooped up some of those eggs with green weenies when it was available that morning.

Los Niños

After church, we continued on our journey beyond the mega-city into the outskirts of civilization, a desert-like region where the children's home was located. This home was where we would spend most of our time. I had never spent any time at an orphanage, so it was a new experience for me. I had no cultural training and no idea what to expect. I was simply feeling my way through the situation.

When we arrived, children flocked around us with a warm, cheerful welcome. We still had our Sunday attire on, which was casual. Nothing fancy. I liked the idea of wearing flip-flops and a cotton t-shirt with a plain, black, cotton skirt. The simplicity of it fit my style.

One of the young girls, perhaps 13 or 14 years old, approached me with curiosity. In her mouth was a Blow Pop® that had stained her tongue bright red. She was ordinary, not particularly attractive. Her hair was somewhat messy. She brushed up against me as she smacked her sucker, and I remember sticky red fingers leaving prints on my white shirt. Culture shock. No one prepared me for what to expect or coached me to let loose and enjoy spending time with the kids. Perhaps they assumed that we knew to do that, but I was feeling my three feet of personal space being violated. My attention was also directed towards the white shirt, one I liked, being ruined with red dye. I couldn't speak with this girl, or with any of the other children for that matter, but I did learn that her name was Angelica. I wasn't sure what to think about her and didn't understand her quiet curiosity. But there were several times she approached me and just smiled.

At first, I felt uneasy with Angelica because I didn't trust myself. I've never handled awkward silence well, and my friends from work knew my reputation for saying the wrong thing at the wrong time. It was one of my unfortunate gifts, and it led to relentless teasing over one particular incident that we called my "Happy Thanksgiving moment."

The moment happened at lunchtime one day near Thanksgiving, when we carpooled together to grab a bite to eat. It was my turn to drive. Caught by a red light, I noticed the homeless guy who frequented the corner with his cardboard sign. I must confess I was really cynical at the time and had little compassion towards beggars on the streets of our city. So I tried to ignore him as he stared blankly in my direction. My friend in the passenger seat pulled out a large bill and told me to roll down the window and give it to him. I didn't want to argue with her, and I felt his eyes peering at me. So I handed him the money. His expression didn't change, and he said nothing. The need to say something in the pregnant pause was overwhelming, and right as the light turned green, I blurted out a cheery "Happy Thanksgiving!" With a smile, off I drove. I was immediately scolded for my awkward insensitivity. Any time thereafter when I said something inappropriate or stupid, my friends would call it a "Happy Thanksgiving moment."

Well aware of my unfiltered tendencies, I was scared to death of what I'd say around Angelica. Not that she would understand any unfortunate mishap, but my English-speaking teammates would.

I began to relax as the week unfolded, and I learned to dispense treats more sincerely and graciously than I had with the beggar. One of the treats we had for the kids was packs of tiny chewing gum squares called Chiclets®. We stored them in our vehicle, and any move we made toward the vehicle tipped them off. They would come running like a flock of chickens towards red toenail polish in a chicken coop. Been there, done that. You'd better be ready to dance when they do. They had clearly done this before, and they knew what we were up to. So when they saw that we had Chiclets®, they went wild. We felt like rock stars as they climbed up our arms trying to get the sugary snacks that we held just beyond their reach.

In the lull of the day, after several hours of entertaining the kids with games and trying to overcome language barriers with charade-like communication, we would busy ourselves preparing lessons and crafts for Vacation Bible School (VBS) while most of the kids took naps during the siesta. It was a quiet time to reflect and process all that we had seen and done in this new culture. It was during this time that I began to realize their infectious laughs and innocent charm had captured my heart.

One little girl, who was about four, came to the screen door of the pavilion where we were assembling VBS materials. She pressed her face against the screen, longing for attention. She smiled, and it was apparent that she wasn't sleepy; she wanted more play time. We returned her smile and sat there focused on the task at hand, while one of the staff redirected her. I relished the quiet moments to catch my breath and recharge my batteries, since I wasn't filled with the same boundless energy the kids had, especially in the heat of the day. In hindsight, I've often regretted not taking that little girl up on the invitation.

Like the little girl, not all kids took advantage of rest in the mid-day hours, and images of infants still in diapers sitting in the breezeway between the buildings feeding themselves from a bottle are burned in my mind. The older kids looked after the younger ones and, while the skeleton crew of staff impressed me with their loving devotion and long days of tireless sacrifice, the truth was that they could only be in so many places and do so many things at one time. I contrasted the infancy of my own daughter — the comforts of her nursery and a loving caregiver to administer every single bottle — with the scene before me. It pulled at my heart.

During the down time, the director of the orphanage had asked for help with his accounting records, and being the bean counter that I was, I offered to take a look. I was impressed with his meticulous records on four-column paper, and I marveled at how closely he monitored the shoestring budget, even going so far as intentionally changing from incandescent light bulbs to LED bulbs to save a few dollars. I had never missed those dollars at home and preferred the instant, bright yellow glow of the incandescent to the slow-starting, cold blue LEDs. But preference was no issue; he only had so much to work with.

After reviewing the records, the director shared a few stories about the backgrounds of the children we had met, and I soaked them in. They were difficult stories. Difficult situations. Situations I was blessed never to have encountered. And the way he loved those children, the way he and his wife devoted their lives to sacrificially care for them, astonished me.

After meeting with the director, I went to sit on a bench in the shaded courtyard that provided protection from the scorching sun. I don't know where all the kids had gone, perhaps to their dorms for naps, but they weren't outside. It was quiet. So when I sat down, I was surprised to see Angelica walking towards me. I scooted over to one end so I wouldn't be hogging the entire bench, and, instead of taking a place at the other end, she sat right next to me. I almost reverted to trying to maintain my three feet of personal space, but, after several days of uninhibited play with the children, I was more at ease with the closeness they craved. Then it surprised me when she locked arms with me and simply rested her head on my shoulder and closed her eyes. Not a word was said. Neither of us attempted to communicate. But more was said to me in that moment than in a week's worth of drawing pictures in the dirt to learn each other's language. Here was a girl who needed love. I didn't know her story, and I probably never would. But judging from the few stories I had heard from the director, she most likely had some scars. Whatever I had not been willing to give her the first day we met, I was more than willing to give her in this moment. It was as if, no matter how clean or dirty I perceived her to be at first, the barriers were gone and I just wanted her to be held and loved by a mom who wouldn't be absent the rest of her life.

Questions filled my mind and my heart pounded with compassion as I held back tears. I closed my eyes, too, and wondered how long she had been there. Was she like the infant who fended for himself in the breezeway, aided only by whichever older child was willing to offer help? What was her story? Oh, how drastically different her childhood must have been from mine.

Good-Bye

Our final night in Mexico was spent at the orphanage with the children. They wanted to surprise our team with a fiesta. Pizza was ordered, an enormous treat for the kids, and I was tickled to see it delivered on motorbikes. There was lively music, we painted their faces, and we celebrated our last night together. I thought of the expression "all good things must come to an end." Night had fallen and we had stayed as late as we could; it was time to say good-bye. It was a bittersweet moment, because I missed my little stinker at home and couldn't wait to wrap her up in my arms again, but I also dreaded telling these children good-bye.

We had been instructed not to make any promises to them, especially ones we couldn't keep. When emotions are running high, it's tempting to say "I'm coming to see you next year," or "I'll write to you," or other "pie crust promises" that are easily broken, so it's best to leave those things unsaid. There is enormous risk of leaving another scar on their hearts if promises aren't followed through. Our farewell would most likely be a permanent good-bye.

In the crowd of laughs and tears and warm hugs, Angelica approached me with tears streaming down her brown, freckled cheeks. We embraced in a big hug. After letting go, she stepped back, pointed to my heart with her finger, and said in a choked voice, "Mi mama." I didn't expect that. I didn't know what was in her mind, or what I did to deserve such a touching sentiment. All I know is this: it broke my heart.

I'm sure that every one of my teammates had similar experiences with children that gravitated towards them all week, because the ride back to the hotel was quiet except for the unavoidable sniffles coming from us all.

Paradigm Shift

Without a doubt, that trip changed me for the rest of my life. I thought I was going to make a contribution to these kids, but I came back with far more of a blessing than whatever meager offerings I took to them.

God became *enormously* bigger to me after visiting Mexico. Our new friends had profound relationships with the same Father I loved. They prayed to the same God I prayed to. He knew them, too, and somehow I felt inexplicably tiny. The song we sang in the service, *He Knows My Name,* was the same song we often sang back home. They knew it too, and it applied to all of us. God loves *all* His children, and I was deeply moved by something I had always heard about but never been an eyewitness to. I saw how His people worshiped so freely and with such passion. There was no pretense as they raised their hands to praise our Father, and how they openly gave Him credit for answered prayers, even the little things they had brought to His feet. I felt the presence of the Holy Spirit like never before.

I loved how they took their only asset, a small block building, and used it to its fullest. It was filled to capacity throughout the entire week, for the sole purpose of serving the community. I thought of how our mega-churches sit empty for the vast portion of the week until the Sunday churchgoers casually showed up for an hour or two on Sunday morning. And I wrestled with that thought as I wondered whether the churches I had attended in America had missed the mark on active service. Why did our churches seem so apathetic?

I came to appreciate another culture and embraced the idea that it's not *wrong*, it's just *different*. I enjoyed the warm-culture aspect of our friends and the high value they placed on relationship and community in comparison to the cold-culture, individualist society I came from.

A flame of passion was ignited. My heart began to beat for missions. I was ready to go home and talk about all I had seen and learned. I was ready to make a radical stand in opposition to the apathy I felt I had been a part of for so long. I was ready to shed the pretense that had smothered me for years. To be set free from that snare. I was ready to be *real*. An open book. To actually do the one thing I thought I had been doing — to follow Christ — with no inhibitions, no matter the cost.

CHAPTER 8:

TOOLS FOR DISCOVERY & DISCUSSION

1. Has your cultural world view ever been challenged? If so, how did this particular challenge change your beliefs?

2. Do you think apathy plagues the American church? Do you think the idea of self-sufficiency has anything to do with how many Americans view worship?

3. Do you ever feel held back from pure worship due to fear of what others would think? (i.e. raising hands in praise during worship service, or being transparent with your prayer requests) How do you think God feels about these inhibitions in His church?

CHAPTER 8: A SEARCH FOR BIBLICAL TRUTH
DIVERSITY AND GOD'S PLAN FOR ALL OF MANKIND

When God chose Israel to be His people, He made an unconditional covenant with Abraham. One of the points of the covenant was that through Abraham all the families of the earth would be blessed. It was through Abraham's lineage that Christ would be sent to fulfill the prophesy as Israel's Redeemer and would become the ultimate blessing (Genesis 12:1-3). However, Christ didn't come only to redeem the Jews in Israel, God's covenant people. Christ also came to redeem any who believed in Him, and that included the Gentiles (anyone not a Jew). Read Galatians 3:6-9.

First, we must understand the old covenant (this one being conditional) that God instituted at Mount Sinai with the Jews. Read Exodus 19:1-8. Verse 5 stated the conditions of the covenant upon which the people agreed. However, did they obey and keep God's commands? No. We have the entire Old Testament to document Israel's rebellion. Therefore, a new covenant (Matthew 26:28, Hebrews 8:1-13) was instituted by Christ as foretold by the prophet Jeremiah in Jeremiah 31:31-34.

Through these covenants we learn that God desires salvation for everyone (Jews and Gentiles). Read Revelation 7:9-17. Verse 9 speaks of a great multitude of all nations standing before God's throne, not just Israel. If we truly understand the patience, loving kindness, and great lengths God has shown in order to redeem all of mankind through His son Jesus, then what do we know about

God's feelings towards diversity and people of different cultures? Does racism, prejudices, or superiority have any place in the body of Christ?

CHAPTER 9

The Tsunami of Divorce

The Dreaded Pop Quiz

No matter what season of life we may find ourselves in, there are always things we can learn about ourselves if we choose to do so. I tend to learn more about myself when I'm fanning my little white flag through the smoke of battle. But what is more important is what we learn about God in these seasons and how we apply the truth once it has been revealed to us.

For a people-pleaser like me, one of the most damaging blows to my ego was discovering that I didn't measure up to another person's expectations. Friend or foe, it didn't matter. There were certain character traits I hoped to portray, and to discover that someone else's perception of me was anything different sent me into a predictable tailspin. That was my pattern.

In his letter to the Galatians, the apostle Paul asks whether we are striving to please men or God. This was a question I had to seriously ponder after arriving home from Mexico. Would I slip easily back into old habits like wearing masks of pretense, hopelessly trying to please others, clinging to weighty bitterness, and shooting forth sharp responses? Or would I surrender to God? I knew I had to make some changes if my life was going to line up more consistently with what I preached, but I found it was difficult to live it out in the face of adversity.

Paul gave us some specific instruction on conduct and behavior.

> "Therefore I urge you, brethren, by the mercies of God, to present your bodies a living and holy sacrifice, acceptable to God, which is your spiritual service of worship."
> Romans 12:1

Because of my call to a deeper devotion to Christ, I was committed to laying those unchecked sins before Him and presenting myself as a living sacrifice. And the more I studied the Old Testament and understood how God required blemish-free sacrifices, the more I was humbled by the gospel of the New Testament, because Jesus became the blemish-free sacrifice that I could never be.

He is wonderful.

He is compassionate.

He is just.

I was, and continue to be, far from blemish-free, but I knew that Jesus covered me with His love and the sacrifice of His perfect blood. And it is only due to my relationship with Him that I could ever present myself a living sacrifice.

The passion kindled within me down in Mexico didn't wane, but it was certainly about to be put to the test. It wasn't going to be easy living out my new resolve.

Isn't it funny the lines of parallel we can draw? Back in school, after we had studied some particular material, some sort of test would be given. Worst of them all was the dreaded pop quiz. At least regular tests were scheduled, so we knew when the teacher would be putting us through the wringer, but pop quizzes always caught us off guard and made our hearts sink.

So here was the material:

I had said I'd follow Christ, no matter the cost, even if no one else followed.

And here was the unanticipated pop quiz:

Separation from spouse and ultimate divorce.

Struck Down by Calamity

When the pop quiz was announced, my heart sank. While you can see a tsunami coming, there's no way to brace for the enormity of the impact.

In 2004, a devastating tsunami in the Indian Ocean pushed miles into the mainland of Sri Lanka. I vividly recall footage of the event on national news, as almost 300,000 people lost their lives in the sweeping waters. Images of trembling children clinging to treetops as their parents and other loved ones washed away are stamped in my mind. Buildings, vehicles, trees ... *everything* surrendered to the force that came upon it, and everything combined in the violent currents added to the destruction, until nothing was left but a wasteland.

I was still a new mother. My daughter wasn't even a year old, and I was experiencing pure delight with her at the moment I saw the tsunami on the news. In fact, I had her swaddled in my arms, snug as a bug against the winter's cold, and I stood in my living room as I watched the *most* chilling image. Another mother halfway around the world also held her baby, except her baby didn't survive the tidal waves. My heart broke for her as I looked down at my vibrant bundle of joy. My baby was staring up at me, all smiles. Her baby was lifeless, limbs hanging, and the look on her face said it all. Her baby wouldn't be smiling up at her again, ever.

I've heard it said that if a picture is worth a thousand words, then an experience is worth a thousand pictures. I'm sure there are a thousand pictures that captured the horror of that day, but it only took one — that one — to etch itself in my mind so I'd never forget.

There have been other, unforgettable catastrophic events in my lifetime. And when these unforeseen calamities collide with us, we never forget where we were and what we were doing. I remember being in the library in elementary school, debating with a fellow classmate about whether Snow White's dress should be white or yellow, just moments before our class gathered to watch the space shuttle launch in 1984; a teacher named Christa McAuliffe was aboard. It must have been an exciting day for all my teachers to see one of their own given the opportunity to venture into space — until the moment the space shuttle exploded. It was horrific for an unsuspecting second grader, and I can't imagine how it affected our teachers. Not only was it a shockingly sad moment in itself, but they had responsibility for a library full of children as all of our eyes were locked on the burning wreckage.

I can also tell you where I was when planes flew into the World Trade Center in New York City on September 11, 2001. I was driving to work when the first plane hit, well before anyone realized the gravity of the situation. The casual report I heard on the radio left me imagining some crazy crop-duster wandering off-course and barely grazing a building with his little prop plane. (As if there were any crop-dusting going on in New York City, but that's where my Mississippi brain took me.) So I dismissed it and surfed the stations until I found some music. It didn't take long for the truth of the terrorist attack to be revealed once I made it to work. The national news had everyone gathered together around any television available. Work was put on hold as we watched life-sized images replay in slow motion on the theatre-like screen in my client's boardroom until the smoldering towers eventually fell one after the other. Graphic images haunted my mind. I was working next to our international airport when it happened, and normally we could hear the constant take-off and landing of commercial jets on the runway across the road. But when all airports were shut down and no noise could be heard, the silence was eerie.

When my catastrophic pop quiz was announced, I went through a tidal wave of emotions. It hit me like a tsunami, and I knew there would be no undoing the destruction by those walls of waves. It was final. There would be no pushing back the water to keep the house standing.

God's Emergency Response

I was overwhelmed. I found myself like the trembling child in the treetop, trying to hang on as the world was swept out from under me. I did my best to maintain reasonable composure for the sake of my daughter and any other unfortunate person that encountered me. After the initial shock wave hit, I sat there, just as I had in the school library, and numbly watched the wreckage burn. It was tragic, but completely out of my control. In response to the tragedy, I shut down, just like the airports on 9/11. The eerie silence took the wind out of my sails, and left me lying on the floor staring at the wall, unable to put one foot in front of the other. The negative response was profound, but it wouldn't be that way for long. God would intervene, just as He always had.

> "Have you not known? Have you not heard? The everlasting God, the Lord, the Creator of the ends of the earth, neither faints nor is weary. His understanding is unsearchable. He gives power to the weak, and to those who have no might He increases strength. Even the youths shall faint and be weary, and the young men shall utterly fall, but those who wait on the Lord shall renew their strength; they shall

mount up with wings like eagles, they shall run and not be weary, they shall walk and not faint." Isaiah 40:28–31

God boldly poured His Word out on me like never before. He wasn't going to let me wallow in my sorrow and fear. He promised to give me power, because I was weak. He promised to increase and renew my strength, because I had no might. He told me to wait on Him. And because I am thick-headed and need to be told something more than once, He kept giving me promises, and hope, and more promises.

> "'Fear not, for I am with you; be not dismayed, for I am
> your God. I will strengthen you, yes, I will help you, I will
> uphold you with My righteous right hand.'" Isaiah 41:10

Who could argue with that? A declaration straight from the mouth of God. When we picture someone being held up, we picture one who is limp, perhaps a wounded warrior with comrades on either side carrying him to the helicopter to be lifted up to safety. The original Hebrew word used for "uphold" in this verse means "to take hold, to maintain and stay up." What a beautiful picture that God would personally come alongside us and give us the power to stand. He knew I would need it, because every time I attempted to stand, I'd wilt back down again. But He has always been right there to pick me up.

My favorite nugget of truth, the one that kept my head above water after the wave hit, was also found in the book of Isaiah, a book I came to love deeply and that has had profound significance to me.

> "'Fear not, for I have redeemed you; I have called you by
> your name; you are Mine. When you pass through the
> waters, I will be with you; and through the rivers, they shall
> not overflow you. When you walk through fire, you shall

not be burned, nor shall the flame scorch you.'"
Isaiah 43:1–2

I must point out that God allows trials in our lives to shape and mold us. So He chooses the word "when" in describing the trials of life. He doesn't say "if"; He says "when." So we can count on trials coming, but we can also count on Him to carry us through them. I wish I could say that I had unshakeable resolve, that it was that simple. But it wasn't. I may have done well academically, but I am a slow student in learning spiritual things. It was a process. I knew it would have to run its natural course as He upheld me each step of the way. I knew He wasn't going to let me drown, but I sure did suck in a lot of water along the way.

A Mix of Joy and Anger

After the initial devastation and subsequent events, I was extremely vulnerable, and my mind played tricks on me. My old routine had been seriously altered, and I would wake up at the same hour every night only to find out that my living nightmare was *not* a dream. On the other hand, vivid nightmares plagued me well into the daylight hours, even when I was awake. Thankfully, those dreams were never really true.

God gave me truth to combat the sleepless nights and the things that perpetuated them.

> "Weeping may endure for a night, but joy comes in the morning." Psalm 30:5

I knew the sleepless nights wouldn't last forever. And although there were nights when I did battle demons, I clung to this verse, prayed over it, and cried different kinds of tears in the morning, tears of joy, as He delivered everything He promised. The things that taunted me were instantaneously resolved the next morning.

During the bouts of sleeplessness, God dealt with me. It was in these quiet hours, in the late-night silence, that I heard Him best. And the first thing that needed to be dealt with was my anger.

"Be angry, and do not sin. Meditate within your heart on your bed, and be still." Psalm 4:4

I was angry. Anger and depression was something I battled for far longer than I want to admit. I didn't understand it; it wasn't officially diagnosed, but it was there. Depression was a living, breathing beast that sucked me into a black hole, a vortex that wouldn't release me until it had devoured every single ounce of my dignity and willpower.

I could physically feel when these spells were coming on, and I felt hopeless to stop them. That angered me even more. While there were things I was reasonably, rightly angry about, I let the anger consume me. It became a gross sin in my life.

The biggest culprit that fed my sinful anger was the need to know *why*. It fanned the flames. I had always sought answers, academically, and I could find an answer to most questions. But this one puzzled me, and I couldn't just Google the answer.

I tried to make a connection from point A to point B and found that I couldn't. It wasn't a straight line. It was fuzzy and convoluted, like a winding country road. Trying to make the connection was like trying to make your way to Grandma's house out in the country by following turn-by-the-rock directions that led you down unmarked dirt roads, only to find out that Cousin Eddy moved most of the rocks some time ago and there are no neighbors to ask for help. Not being able to make the connection frustrated me.

One day I was trying to tidy the house at the last minute, and I unfairly snapped at my daughter as she stood anxiously looking out the front door waiting for our company to arrive. She calmly looked at me and asked, "Momma, why are you so angry?"

I replied, "Baby, I'm not angry at you. I've just got a lot on my mind that you wouldn't understand."

She instantly rebutted, "I understand, Momma. Your heart's been broke, but Jesus said we should pray for those who persecute us." And then she went straight back to looking out the front door, as if what she had said to me was as insignificant as asking to play with her favorite toy.

She was five years old, and, yes, she is a walking, talking miracle. God has used her to reach people in ways we will never be able to count. But I *never* had her memorize that particular verse from Matthew 5:44. It was a powerful God-moment as He intervened, *again*, to speak truth into my life using my daughter as His mouthpiece. He knew I was angry, and he kept telling me to be on my knees in prayer. The more I prayed about my anger and the need to know *why*, the more He released me from the burden of it all. He revealed that I didn't need to know why. I simply needed to trust Him and what He was doing in my life. So I let that part go.

After my daughter had so pointedly called me out about my anger, I was ashamed that I was letting it get the best of me. I knew she was watching me, and so were a whole lot of other people, for that matter. I had a testimony to uphold, because so many eyes were watching to see how we would walk through these flames. But I had already been assured that I wasn't going to be scorched, even if I was dumb enough to run back into the burning house to sit and stew every now and then.

Building a Legacy

My resolve to raise my daughter up in the ways of the Lord was stronger than ever. I took every opportunity I could throughout the day to point her to Him, to show her how He manifests Himself in every facet of creation and our daily lives. It was my mission.

I wanted a legacy of spiritual depth for her. I wanted to spare her from the dumb mistakes I had made, and the best way to combat that was to give her spiritual insight and a firm foundation through the wisdom and power of the Holy Spirit. I was dedicated to tearing down any behaviors in my life not consistent with the Christian faith; I wanted her to see a life wholly dedicated to the Lord.

We prayed together because I intentionally wanted her to see me pray aloud on my knees before Almighty God. If the tears and snot came, then so be it. It was all part of shedding the pretense I had carried for so many years. I wanted my prayers to be real. To be fervent. I wanted to teach her how to pray and tell God everything.

I had tucked her in one night, on one of the rare occasions I allowed music to sing her to sleep, and as I knelt beside the bed to pray with her, MercyMe's *Bring the Rain* came on the radio. Here are the lyrics:

"I can count a million times
People asking me how I
Can praise You with all that I've gone through
The question just amazes me
Can circumstances possibly
Change who I forever am in You
Maybe since my life was changed
Long before these rainy days
It's never really ever crossed my mind
To turn my back on You, oh Lord
My only shelter from the storm
But instead I draw closer through these times
So I pray
Bring me joy, bring me peace
Bring the chance to be free
Bring me anything that brings You glory
And I know there'll be days
When this life brings me pain
But if that's what it takes to praise You
Jesus, bring the rain."

These words expressed how I truly felt, and that song was our tearful prayer that night. God was carrying us through the storm, people were watching, and if He got the *most* glory by our giving Him praise with inexplicable joy in a seemingly impossible situation, then I wanted Jesus to keep bringing the rain.

Priceless Support Superior to Two Cents

It was interesting to see the varying reactions people had to my pop quiz. Some were good. Some were bad. Some were predictable. Some were shocking. One thing was certain, the division rippled into various relationships. Battle lines were drawn, and, unfortunately, some people felt the need to choose a side.

My parents always stood by my side to support me. They lived only about five minutes away, and Daddy began calling me to see if I was okay or needed anything. To this day, Daddy will call me before he goes out to work in the yard, gets on his tractor, or gets ready to do anything that will put him out of pocket, just to see if I'm okay or if there's any chance I'd need him.

One day I did. I still had a garage full of my ex-husband's "toys" that had not vacated the premises, and I was trying to get the yard mowed for the last time that year. There was one problem. The riding mower was parked all the way in the back, behind a big motorcycle. There was no way to get the mower out of the garage except to move the motorcycle. I knew it was way too heavy for me to ride, but I reasoned that if I straddled it and walked it back far enough out of the way, then surely I could keep it balanced, and then I'd be able to retrieve the mower.

I didn't.

The lipstick-red motorcycle was brand new and only one payment had been made on it before the pop quiz had been sprung. And my straddle strategy was not a solid solution. The motorcycle came crashing down as I lost my balance. The brand new, shiny chrome pipes scuffed on the hard floor — and so did my leg.

It was a brief moment of defeat, and on any normal day my strong will and stubborn pride would have bristled and *might* have allowed me to muster enough strength to hoist that bike back up on its kickstand, but instead I sprawled out on the cold concrete and sobbed as I reached for the phone. When Daddy answered, it only took a sniffle before he said he was on his way. I don't think I even said anything, and in five minutes flat he was there to make it all better, and pick up the motorcycle.

The same support was true of my sweet Grandpa. We had all gathered for Thanksgiving, just weeks after the tsunami hit me, and most everybody was laughing and enjoying each other's company. Actually, I think I was the only one who wasn't. But nothing needed to be said about the elephant in the room, and it didn't have to be an open family affair.

In the driveway that night, my grandpa came to hug me and say good-bye, and even though we had hardly exchanged a word that night, he stood before me with the sweetest eyes of grace and said something profoundly simple, "It won't always be like this." I've applied his words of wisdom to a multitude of stinky situations since that time.

On the other end of the spectrum were the people who callously spewed their ignorant opinions, which only tempted me to the anger that lay just beneath the surface.

One day at work, I was having a bad day emotionally, so I had taken advantage of the luxury of closing my office door so that I could work between the sniffles without worrying about passers-by. There were several days I had to do that. But this one day, a co-worker from a different department, one that I almost never had to interact with, must have gotten fed up with my closed-door policy. He made a point of stopping by my office to tell me that I needed to check my emotions at the door before I came to work. I resented his lack of compassion for a long time, because he was a professed believer, and I knew he had never walked a mile in my shoes. I prayed he never would.

Contentment with Lessons Learned

I recall having a heart-to-heart talk with one of my dear friends. She had just endured emotional pain from a miscarriage and I was in the midst of my pop quiz, but we laughed together as we shared some of the shockingly stupid things that people, church people, actually said to us as they attempted to console us.

Usually I was the person with no filter, but God allowed me to experience a taste of my own medicine. Like me, most people didn't intend to be mean-spirited. Wrong things get said even when people want to say something helpful. I've learned that sometimes the best thing to say is nothing at all. A hug, a smile, a shoulder to cry on, listening ears, a clean tissue, all are far better alternatives to saying the wrong thing. And if the Lord hasn't put it on your heart, it's best to keep it to yourself.

I've also learned the importance of forgiveness, whether the object of my forgiveness is a pop quiz and all that it entails or an unfiltered opinion at the office. I realized that there would be no way I could stand before a Holy God one day and expect His forgiveness if I was never willing to offer it to anyone else. It would be an Isaiah moment, where I stand convicted and my only response is "Woe is me!" True forgiveness is possible. I have experienced it. I have given it. And I knew the exact moment when I was supernaturally able to say those words, mean it, and physically feel the weight lifted off of me. It is freeing beyond words. The apostle Paul says it best.

> "Therefore, as the elect of God, holy and beloved,
> put on tender mercies, kindness, humility, meekness,
> longsuffering; bearing with one another, and forgiving one
> another, if anyone has a complaint against another; even as
> Christ forgave you, so you also must do. But above all these
> things put on love, which is the bond of perfection. And let
> the peace of God rule in your hearts, to which also you were

called in one body, and be thankful."
Colossians 3:12–15

I found peace with my pop quiz. Contentment.

I wanted to be a living sacrifice, and, when I made that commitment, I wondered what it would cost me. I may have lost some significant things by the world's standards, but most of what I lost needed to go.

Hypocrisy.

Bitterness.

Unforgiveness.

It felt good to let them go. But would I ever be foolish enough to pick these things back up again? Being a living sacrifice requires dying to ourselves daily, asking the Holy Spirit to fill our lives and lead us each step of the way. Of course it would be possible to step on another snare if I'm living apart from the help of the Holy Spirit, but at least I'd know how to get out of it the next time around. And while the tragic experience of divorce is one I'd never wish upon anyone, I would never want to undo it and end up forsaking the richest truths I've ever learned about myself and my Savior in that chapter of my life.

This particular chapter had ended, and I was about to begin a new one. A quote from the movie *The Lord of the Rings: The Return of the King* best described that transition of my life. Frodo Baggins has destroyed the ring that burdened him for so long. He is weary from battling the evil forces that hunted and haunted him, and as he returns to his home, he wonders, "How do you pick up the threads of an old life? How do you go on when, in your heart, you begin to understand there is no going back? There are some things that time cannot mend. Some hurts that go too deep, that have taken hold."

I was changed — forever changed, and in more ways than I could quantify. God was growing me exponentially, but even so, it wouldn't be an easy road ahead. There would be more trial and temptation, and the enemy was fast on my heels to target my weak spots, discredit my testimony, and camouflage the snares he set before me as never before. I was an easy target the first time around, hopping directly onto the most visible, rusty traps, but the enemy was going to have to up the ante and work a little harder to catch me the next go around.

CHAPTER 9:

TOOLS FOR DISCOVERY & DISCUSSION

1. What tsunamis have swept you off your feet? Did you search for an answer to explain "why" it happened?

2. What angers you? Do you confess your anger or let it turn to bitterness? What core feelings (hurt, fear, loneliness, sadness) trigger your anger? Have you experienced true forgiveness for something you did horribly wrong? Have you forgiven others for something horribly wrong done to you? What does God say about unwillingness to forgive?

3. What does it mean to be a living sacrifice and die to yourself daily?

CHAPTER 9: A SEARCH FOR BIBLICAL TRUTH

ANGER & BITTERNESS

Anger often shows what we are passionate about defending. It's okay to be angry at times for the right reasons. Is your anger a righteous anger? Are the things that anger you caused by violations of God's commands? Ephesians 4:26 tells us to be angry, but do not sin. We are God's image bearers, and anger is an emotion not only created by Him, but also felt by Him. We know that sin angers God too. So, anger shouldn't be frowned upon when it is used appropriately. However, we shouldn't remain in anger. The anger we hold onto only gives the devil a foothold and an opportunity to wreak havoc in our lives. Anger can easily turn into bitterness, an unhealthy byproduct of unconfessed hurts, fears, loneliness, or sadness. We are to confess our anger and give it to God, trusting Him to do His job and fix what is wrong.

Forgiveness also plays a significant role. What does Psalm 37:8 instruct us to do? What about Proverbs 19:11? We have a choice to use our discretion to forgive our offenders and release the worry that binds us. Unforgiveness can intensify our bitterness. Life has never been easy since Adam and Eve sinned in the Garden and God rebuked them with His curse (Genesis 3:13-19). The writer of Hebrews knew this and encouraged believers in Hebrews 12:12-15 to press on, pursue peace, and self examine so that bitterness does not creep in. Proverbs 14:10 says the heart knows the bitterness that lies within even if no one else has a clue about what troubles us. So what can we do if we find ourselves in this condition? Read 1 John 1:9. Confession and forgiveness must be daily practices for every believer. Give your worries and hurts to God. Trust that He will heal you and work it out in His time.

CHAPTER 10

Rediscovery

Turning the Page

My grandpa was right. Life wasn't always like it had been in the aftermath of the flood. Frodo was right too. There are some things that time truly cannot mend. While time can help heal a wound with the loving grace of the Father, a scar still remains. And only time would tell the potential those scars would have to affect me.

As the waters receded and life resumed, I pondered the things I had learned. I began to appreciate the quiet evenings after I had put my daughter to bed. It was a time to snuggle up in my cozy chair and have uninterrupted one-on-one time with the Lord. I identified with King David as he looked back on his trials.

"Unless Your law had been my delight,
I would have perished in my affliction." Psalm 119:92

That is exactly how I felt. God's Word carried me through the storm, and His promises unfolded just as He said they would. I didn't drown, and I didn't get scorched by the flame. I came through it stronger. And that was exactly what God intended.

He blessed me with a large fellowship of believers at the church where I had put down roots. In times of trouble, I realized how much I appreciated them. They were there for me. They met my needs. They did what a church was supposed to do. They rallied around me, and I could never put a price tag on the relationships formed during those struggles.

I had been in a couples' class at church and, even though my newfound single status made me feel like I should transfer to a ladies' class, they wouldn't let me leave. We had endured too much together. All of my friends said that Jesus is now my Husband, so I was still part of a couple and there was no need to leave. I was relieved, because I really wasn't looking forward being separated from them. I needed them too much.

But since I, like Frodo, had been changed, I saw things from a whole new perspective. I had been humbled. Quieted. I spent more time listening, observing, and soaking things in. And one of the things I noticed about couples was that they squabbled over the most insignificant things. Whether it was wet towels left on the bathroom floor, or underwear here, there, and everywhere, or battles over the remote, or burnt offerings for dinner, the nagging complaints seemed so meaningless and silly. And I knew I had been guilty of it too.

The good thing about surviving adversity and the change it brings is that one is less likely to judge others. I'm a firm believer that seasoned Christians who have been tested are the least likely to cast judgment. It's the believer who has taken a long look in the mirror and sees a natural-born sinner, guilty to the core apart from the blood of Jesus, who realizes that his sin is just as great as the next person's. One of the benefits I reaped from my adversity was a dead Pharisee. That part of me, the judgmental hypocrisy, had died and been washed away by the tsunami. Good riddance.

So I had no judgment for towels on the floor and such. Although I understood my friends' irritation, I couldn't understand why those types of battles ever made it to the battlefield. But I was not going to condemn them for it. I had learned that some things just aren't worth fussing over. Life's too short to spend it fighting all the time. I was relieved that my fighting had stopped. And I carried a conviction to tell my story, because I knew there was no way in Hades every single marriage in that class was as perfect as they pretended to be. I knew they fought like cats and scrappy dogs during the week, then put on a mask for Sunday worship, just like I did.

God had cured me of my pretense, and any indication of it in others sickened me. Not the people who did it, because I loved them, but the fact that our culture had so preconditioned us to believe we must handle life alone, and that it's shameful to be less than perfect. How can the church ever be the church and function the way it's intended, how can it love and nurture, if half the folks walking around ain't tellin' the truth? I missed Mexico and the candor they shared as a body of Christ. So I spoke out. And it became easier for me to talk about God and how He had so powerfully drawn me in, carried me through the storm, and given me a heart for missions.

I talked about it at work, and I longed for coffee breaks with fellow believers where we could just sit and talk about Jesus. One sweet friend could tell when the day had gotten long for me, and she would say, "C'mon, let's go have some hot tea. I'll make it for you." She would just be a listening ear and an enormous source of encouragement with a smile that could warm the coldest of rooms. I craved that time in the little break room, because I got to spend time with a dear friend and talk about what had become most important to me.

The more God became a part of my everyday conversation, the more I realized others had noticed. They began to come to my office to talk, to download, to cry, to ask for prayer over their struggles. I discovered the joy in being real and sharing life with others.

Testing New Waters

I was rediscovering myself and, in my newfound freedom, I asked myself why I kept doing things a certain way. Was it because that was the way I always did it to please another person? Had I gotten so lost in trying to please others that I had no idea what it was I enjoyed?

Without a doubt, Jesus became my premier interest. But there were other things I discovered I liked too. I found out that I liked movies. I could have counted on one hand the number of times I had gone to the movies in the previous ten years or so. It was rare because I never wanted to go by myself. But when I gave it a try again, I found that a bucket of popcorn, a box of Butterfinger bites, a large Coke, and a plush chair before an enormous screen with the most unreal surround sound was a fantastic outlet of entertainment.

On the contrary, I discovered that I still enjoyed outdoor sportsman activities, but not nearly as much as I had convinced myself in the past. Daddy showed me the joy in these things as a child and I grew up loving the great outdoors, but I grew to loathe the industry for tapping into our culture with ingenious marketing strategies and, once again, successfully conditioning our society to believe that one had to have the top-of-the-line everything to participate in outdoor sports. It never ended. There would always be a newer, better something, and the ease of access and rising price of equipment just about pushed the average blue-collar Joe out of the sport of hunting. It was an obsession, and one that burnt me out. Much like the pretension I had come to hate, this only felt like another flavor of it, and it turned me off. I'd still go hunting or fishing on occasion with my dad or brother, and we'd have a great time. But it was refreshing to be relieved of any pressure, outside or self-induced, to leave my toasty bed on a day off, well before the sun rose, to chase an obsession, and possibly a deer too. It just didn't matter that much to me anymore.

Aside from giving up an expensive hobby, I made other adjustments. As a single parent with essentially the same bills, my budget changed. I finally realized that having a bigger house wasn't all that. But I was stuck with it, at least for the time being. I still loved my home, but it no longer felt like the dream home I had made it out to be years before. It was everything I had wanted, but now, with tainted memories, it felt hollow.

My buddy Cotton was a great companion, and every time I moved from one room to another he would follow, plop back down in a ball next to my feet, and cut his eyes up at me with wrinkly eyebrows and a sigh, as if to tell me, "Would you *please* find a spot and sit still?" I started calling him my shadow, and he would never understand how thankful I was for his loyalty.

Taking New Adventures

That summer, my parents were taking my grandmother and their fifth-wheel camper to Colorado and asked me and my daughter to go. I accepted the invitation and asked if Cotton could go, too, because it just wouldn't feel right to leave him behind. I had never traveled with him before, and I wondered why, in all of my years of preoccupation with other things, I had never considered it.

He made an excellent travel companion on the long road trip, and was happy as a pig in mud when he, my daughter, and I all snuggled up in one big pile of blankets on a pallet on the floor each night. I had never allowed him on the furniture or in the beds because his black fur shed so much, but I thought I might have to reconsider when I got home. I had been more concerned with keeping the couches clean than extending a few simple pleasures to my old friend. I didn't realize until we were on those cold, alpine slopes what a great cuddle-bug he made.

I was relishing a few simple pleasures of my own. The stars were bigger and brighter than they were at home. They begged to be noticed. And the sweet smell of sage filled the cool, crisp air instead of smog and humidity. Mountain flowers peppered the landscape and were a bouquet of beauty for the eyes in comparison to the trash that littered our Southern streets. Cotton and I took long walks down to the crystal clear lake and let our senses soak in all that was around. He retrieved sticks until he wore me out. Then we would head back to the camper to join our family around a fire and tell the silliest of tales to my gullible offspring.

Of all my trips to Colorado, that one became very special to me. Its timing was perfect. We needed it. The pace was slow. And the refreshment it lent was like medicine to the soul.

Stepping Back to Simplicity

The simplicity of the time spent away from home made me yearn for a long-ago era. It reminded me of my great-grandmother and the life she led in a small farmhouse on a Missouri dairy farm. We kids could run a complete circle through the tiny house, as all the rooms were connected, and we could chase each other in and out of screen doors on opposite ends of the wrap-around porch. We were totally freaked out by the musty-smelling cellar down below.

I can still smell chicken frying on the old, white, gas stove, and I can taste the thick, fresh milk or ice cold Tang® that she kept in the fridge. She was an extraordinary cook, and we figured out that her humble kitchen was the best place to congregate.

Everything Grandma owned was simple. She didn't have fancy dishes. In fact, many of her dishes came out of a Super Suds® detergent box. Why did they put glassware treats in odd places like a box of detergent during the post-war era? I'm sure I'll never know. I didn't live through that time of rationing and frugality. The only thing I ever found in a box was a tattoo in my Cracker Jacks. But I inherited a cabinet full of the gems that great-grandma had collected over the years, and they made quite the contrast to the premier pottery and fine china I had sought to collect.

The nostalgic ideal of a Norman Rockwell time period appealed to me more and more. Simplicity called. And I began to think more about it, even when Mom and I went to craft fairs (an annual tradition) and retro-aprons had become a big hit. I wanted one, of course, but with those trendy new aprons and all their trimmings came a trendy price tag. In typical fashion, Momma advised me not to buy one because "that would be so easy to make." And my typical rebuttal was that by the time we hunted down the perfect material, which would, no doubt, be the most expensive bolt of fabric in the store, and spent all our time (and by that I really meant *her* time) sewing it together, I'd have been just as well off to have bought the thing at the craft fair! However, as promised, she did make me one — and in perfect time for holiday cooking.

I proudly wore my apron and thought of my grandmother and of simpler times. I also thought how wonderful it would be if we had an apron in life that shielded us. One we could just toss in the wash when life got messy. Underneath we'd still look flawless, like June Cleaver, and we wouldn't have stains left behind from any unexpected explosions. And while I realized there was no literal apron that could do that, I knew Jesus was the One who filled that purpose in my life. Looking back, I could see how He covered me from a multitude of messes. Many of them whipped up from my own little tattered recipe of destruction, a recipe I was willing to trash.

The changes in me made me smile as I let go of the shinier things I once pursued. I recalled a scene from one of my favorite western sagas, *Lonesome Dove*. Gus was offering words of wisdom to console a much younger friend, Lorie, who was desperate to get out of the dusty, one-saloon, cow town and see firsthand the riches of the big city she had heard so much about, but an opportunity to leave never seemed to happen. She wept in hopelessness. He grinned and gently advised, "Lorie darlin', life in San Francisco, you see, is still just life. If you want any one thing too badly, it's likely to turn out to be a disappointment. The only healthy way to live life is to learn to like all the little everyday things."

I loved Gus's advice, and because of a budget that had shrunk, I was relieved that I had embraced more humble offerings. I often laughed at my simple selections in the grocery-store checkout line as

I shopped for one and a half. My daughter didn't eat much, and she was a picky eater — she only ate about five different things at the time — so I found it hard to cook for one adult without eating the same thing four days in a row. My daughter's appetite for processed, prepackaged items left me compromising with easier meals to cook. Seeing my selections approaching the cashier on the conveyor belt made me feel like a perfect display of singleness. But they fit the budget, and I was completely content.

The following Christmas also had meager offerings. It was like having a sad, little, Charlie Brown Christmas tree with only a few presents under it for my daughter, but, like the vacation we had taken that summer, it became a priceless memory. It was modest. It was quiet. Uneventful in comparison to past celebrations. But it was my favorite. It was a sweet time talking to my precious daughter about celebrating Jesus, just me and her. I thought of the mother in Mexico who was thankful she could buy a single gift for her child's birthday, and I finally knew how she felt.

Learning to Be Alone

Life was much quieter, and another thing I began to notice about this chapter of my life was how God moved people out of my circle. It was a process necessary to prepare me for another lesson He had in store for me, a deeper relationship with Him.

During this process, I simultaneously learned a different lesson: how my scars would begin to affect me. Enormous insecurity plagued me, and as God began moving people away and as fewer people I trusted were available at my beck and call, I grew fearful. I wondered if I had said or done something to cause this newfound distance, but I now know that God had a higher purpose. I am sure my neediness grew wearisome for a select few, but God was showing me that I needed to rely on Him alone. I liked the convenience of being able to pick up a phone and call someone when something weighed on my mind. I liked the feel of a hug when it was needed. I liked my senses: see, hear, smell, touch, and taste. God gave them to me, so they were good. But it was my *faith* He wanted to grow. If you could see it or touch it, then it wouldn't be faith. So my reliance upon tangible things, primarily relationships, would need some tweaking.

I really struggled with this at first. I spent time with God and enjoyed every minute of it. But I wasn't letting Him fill every little crack and crevice within me, the ones that caused me to yearn for other things. So when close relationships began to fade into distant ones, I battled loneliness. As this emotion became more prominent, I became acutely aware of all the couples that seemed to be around me. I felt single. And my insecurity made me feel rejected, as if I had "divorced" stamped in bright red letters on my forehead. Everywhere I looked I saw pairs. My daughter was the joy of my life, but she was my child; it wasn't the same as having a plus-one to share life with. And Cotton couldn't be my plus-one, as much as I enjoyed his company and the fact that we never argued. He and I got along famously.

Loneliness struck. But as always, God responded.

A Call to Deeper Devotion

One evening after tucking my daughter into bed, and Cotton, too, I spent some time with my real plus-one, Jesus, just before I went to bed. I opened my Bible, and I was confronted by the command God gave to Moses, to love the Lord your God with all your heart, with all your soul, and all your strength. I loved God, but that night's devotion time prodded me with the question, *how much?*

I read a familiar passage in a new light. In this particular passage, Jesus had already been crucified, buried, and resurrected, and He had reappeared to the disciples three times when he confronted Simon Peter."

> So when they had eaten breakfast, Jesus said to Simon Peter, 'Simon, son of Jonah, do you love Me more than these?' He said to Him, 'Yes, Lord; You know that I love You.' He said to him, 'Feed My lambs.' He said to him

again a second time, 'Simon, son of Jonah, do you love Me?'
He said to Him, 'Yes, Lord; You know that I love You.'
He said to him, 'Tend My sheep.' He said to him the third
time, 'Simon, son of Jonah, do you love Me?' Peter was
grieved because He said to him the third time, 'Do you love
Me?' And he said to Him, 'Lord, You know all things; You
know that I love You.' Jesus said to him, 'Feed My sheep.'"
John 21:15–17

Like Peter, I was grieved as I had an "aha!" moment with the
Lord regarding the depth of my devotion towards Him. I couldn't
shirk the way this question was directed towards me.

Let's do a fast word study to understand the depth of what was
said in the original Greek language and why I was so convicted that
night. Without understanding the original, the meaning of this passage is almost impossible to see in our English translation.

You see, our English language uses one word for *love*. This passage, in its original Greek context, uses two distinct words for love,
words that have different meanings. Let's face it, we throw the word
love around for a multitude of things: relationships, potato chips,
horses, iPhones. But what did Jesus mean when He asked Peter if he
loved Him? What was Jesus referring to when he asked if Peter loved
Him more than "these"? What was Peter's response? What did Jesus
instruct him to do?

Super fast word study:

Agapao/agape (love) – a total commitment; unselfish and
ready to serve charitably; an affection or benevolence; seeks
the opportunity to do good to all and for the welfare of all;
to dote over; to love

Phileo (love) – tender affection; fond of; to be a friend to

Bosko (tend/feed) – to nourish; to provide food

Poimaino (tend/shepherd) – to act as a shepherd (spiritually), supervisor; *includes* feeding, which is a primary need, but goes beyond to secondary acts like discipline, restoration, and offering material assistance.

So let's revisit those three verses in a clearer context.

Verse 15:

Jesus: Do you *agape* Me more than *these* things?
(Peter, will you give Me total commitment, become my disciple, and not go back to your old way of life? A common interpretation for *"these"* refers to Peter going back to his old job of being a fisherman instead of continuing his calling to be a disciple and fisher of men.)

Peter: Of course I *phileo* You.
(Aw, Jesus, You know I love you like a brother.)

Jesus: *Bosko* My lambs.
(Feed young converts the Word of God.)

Verse 16

Jesus: Do you *agape* Me?
(How about giving Me total commitment, Peter?)

Peter: Of course I *phileo* You.
(Aw, Jesus, You know I love you like a brother.)

Jesus: *Poimaino* My sheep.
(Feed and lead My believers. It's a little more responsibility.)

Verse 17

Peter is now grieved and beginning to grasp the concept...

Jesus: Do you *phileo* Me?
(You obviously haven't made total commitment towards Me yet, so how about brotherly affection instead?)

Peter: Sigh, yes, I *phileo* You.
(I understand my heart better now. I've given you brotherly affection, and although I want to sacrificially follow You, I simply haven't done that yet.)

Jesus: *Bosko* My lambs.
(You're not yet ready for the full responsibility I have laid out for you as a spiritual leader, so let's start by feeding My believers the Word of God and we'll get there.)

Jesus met Peter exactly where he was. He didn't condemn him. He didn't expect Peter to go to seminary and have several degrees before He called him to service. Jesus wanted to use him and knew the plans He had for him. Even though Peter had previously denied Him and still hadn't given Him total commitment, we learn in subsequent versus that Jesus patiently instructed Peter, *"Follow Me."*

That night, I wept and grieved as Peter had done as I had to be completely honest with myself. When God instructed us to love Him with all our heart, soul, and strength in Deuteronomy 6:5, the Hebrew word for love that He chose was equivalent in meaning to the Greek word *agape*: total commitment and devotion. Like Peter, and up to that point, I really believed I loved Jesus whole-heartedly, but was I willing to do *anything* to follow Him?

He was asking ... and I had to give an answer.

CHAPTER 10:

TOOLS FOR DISCOVERY & DISCUSSION

1. What scars remain that affect your daily life? In what ways?

2. Are you a people pleaser? Do you do things that you enjoy or mostly things that others enjoy in an attempt to make them happy?

3. Have you battled loneliness? Have you considered it as God's call for a deeper devotion with Him?

4. How would you honestly describe your love for God, agape or phileo? If phileo, what things are you hesitant to sacrifice to follow Him completely? Do you fear that the loss of whatever you're holding on to won't be filled with the joy and peace of God?

CHAPTER 10: A SEARCH FOR BIBLICAL TRUTH

LONELINESS

Jesus experienced loneliness. When we are lonely, we crave relationship with others. After all, God created us in His image (Genesis 1:26), and He exists as three distinct persons of the Godhead commonly known as the Trinity: God the Father, God the Son, and God the Holy Spirit, all in perfect relationship. Not only are we called to have relationship with God our creator, we are also designed to be in intimate relationship with others. So when we feel lonely, it is natural to want others to be close to us. Jesus demonstrated this in the Garden of Gethsemane prior to His crucifixion and bearing God's wrath as punishment for the sins of the world. His sacrifice and redemption were parts of God's plan from the beginning, so it was no surprise that He would bear God's wrath on the cross. Read Matthew 26:36-46. In His deepest distress and sorrow, Jesus longed to have His closest friends near Him. Repeatedly, they fell asleep and left Him alone. Incarnate Jesus, fully God and fully man bound by flesh and humanity, understood loneliness.

In another example, the Old Testament records miracles performed through the prophet Elijah. Even after seeing God do the impossible, Elijah still found himself alone, fearful, and depressed. Read 1 Kings 19:1-18. What did Elijah want to do in verse 4? Who appeared to him and cared for him in verses 5 and 7? Despite angelic attempts to nurture and sustain him, Elijah chose to withdraw to a cave to be alone. What was asked of him in verse 9? It was the same type of question God asked Adam after sinning in the Garden (Genesis 3:9). These questions were asking where these men were at emotionally and spiritually. They were rhetorical questions, of course, because God already knew the answer. He needed them to understand their shame, fear, and despair because that brought them to the point where they felt the need to hide themselves from God and others. Hiding (physically or emotionally) hinders intimate relationship, one of the very reasons we were created.

What did Elijah hear in verse 12? God did not leave Elijah in his misery. It was the still small voice of the creator that comforted him and showed him he was not alone. God promises in Deuteronomy 31:6 that He will never leave us alone even if we attempt to run to the ends of the earth to escape or hide. He is there.

CHAPTER 11

Yes, Lord

Fig Leaf Moment

Only a short time passed before the next divine appointment occurred. At the most unlikely time. And in the most unlikely place. It was a quiet evening at home. I was soaking in a whirlpool tub full of bubbles, and candles flickered around me as I slumped down into the warm water and closed my eyes. The world simply melted away. It was peaceful. Nothing was on my mind. Nothing was stirring within me. Nothing negative plagued me. It was just a quiet time of nothing.

And just as Peter had gone fishing and unexpectedly had a visitor, so did I. Jesus met me right where I was. His presence became distinct as I recalled our last significant encounter, and the question He presented still loomed. I wanted to run from it, to keep postponing my answer, but there was something so symbolic about being fully exposed, just as Adam and Eve had been in the Garden of Eden. Had I not been so consumed with Him in the moment, I probably would have thought, *"Where is my fig leaf?"* But there was no time for silly antics and, just like Adam and Eve, I couldn't run from my sin or ignore my Creator, who had begun a conversation with me.

The conversation was quite simple. There was no need for flowery words or beating around the bush. It was as if He presented one more question to me: *"Well?"*

I was so thankful to have Peter's example recorded in Scripture. Because in my heart I knew that I had denied Jesus so many times, just as Peter had done. I felt inadequate to answer His calling with complete abandon. But so did Peter. I was comfortable fishing, like Peter, but only for things that had no eternal value. To become a fisher of men would put me way out of my comfort zone, and it scared the pants off of me. But there was one thing that scared me more —God.

It was undeniable. He had brought me far enough and given me enough foundational belief through trial and circumstance that whatever He was asking of me, I knew He wouldn't leave me hanging. He wouldn't take me out into the desert, flip me a quarter, and tell me to call me someone who cared. That was not His character.

My response was just as simple as His question... "Yes, Lord." And it was so profound that it answered a host of other questions that lingered in my mind.

Do you love Me?

In spite of wavering commitment, will you follow Me?

Even if it means giving up some of your comforts and pleasures?

Are you willing to die to self to follow Me?

Will you feed My lambs?

And shepherd My sheep?

Will you trust Me to take you out of your comfort zone, teach you, and place you in this service?

I wept as I climbed out of the tub, wrapped myself in a terry-cloth fig leaf, and dropped to my knees on the floor. Several times I said aloud "Yes, Lord," as tears of joy poured down my cheeks. In that moment, I was utterly filled with the joy that only the Holy Spirit can provide. It engulfed me, and I couldn't wait to share my encounter with others. That encounter might seem insignificant to some. But for me, it was a defining moment, just as it had been for the many people in Scripture who had undeniably come face to face with the Holy One. It truly was one of those experiences that one must experience oneself to understand the depth of what had just happened.

The first stop on my list would be at Momma and Daddy's house. The next morning, I went over for a cup of coffee and declared that I had something to tell them. I'm pretty sure I failed to give the proper sequence of events, which began with the *"Do you love Me?"* dialogue and was followed by the fig leaf incident. I'm also sure I didn't articulate how that question had loomed in my mind. How much I had chewed on it. And why my ultimate submission had such significance. All I could say was that I had a "Yes, Lord" moment.

My dad, a believer, stood across from me on the other side of the kitchen island and looked at me intently. I felt my coffee getting cold in the awkward silence. Again, I don't do awkward silences well, and I'm thankful that another Happy Thanksgiving blooper didn't ruin the moment. It may have been only a single second, but I felt like I was in the hot seat for an eternity with my parents' eyes fixed on me, primarily my dad's, as he studied what it was I was trying to say. I squirmed. It was equivalent in awkwardness to the announcement that I was pregnant with my daughter. I was married, established, and there was absolutely nothing to be ashamed of except that it implied certain things. And that made me uneasy. Of all the things

I could speak freely about to them, there were some things we *never* spoke of, and I was sure they knew babies didn't come from a stork. But I had to bite the bullet and get over my goofy fears.

Thankfully, they asked no questions in the stork moment; Momma squealed with excitement, and I avoided making eye contact with Daddy. I had always been Daddy's little girl and had never made such a monumental announcement before, so I didn't really know what to do with myself. Without a doubt, he was just as excited as my momma.

Although my "Yes, Lord" moment was a completely different set of circumstances than having a baby, I still struggled to compose myself, and I was as jumpy as a cat on a hot tin roof inside. I realized I wasn't making much sense to them, and that made me even more nervous. It only amplified when Dad gruffly asked, "What does that mean?" I kept saying that I didn't know, and I'm sure my ambiguity confused them even more. But I honestly didn't know. I just knew it was big. Whatever it was.

They were fully aware of the work God was doing in my life, and they were in full support of it. But I think it struck fear in them when they could see something much bigger was upon the horizon. I was a single mom. I had just survived the tsunami of divorce. And my parents were concerned that volatility blanketed whatever I was about to tell them. But honestly, those things had nothing to do with my answer. I wasn't wallowing in pity, and no woe-is-me feelings were ever factored into the equation.

To top it off, they may have thought I was going to donate all my clothes, weave a grass skirt, and go join a tribe in the plains of Africa with their firstborn grandchild who happened to have special needs that demanded top-notch medical care — medical care that surely wasn't available in the remotest regions of the world. They knew what the trip to Mexico had done for me. They knew I was wildly passionate about missions. And they knew that it was not unrealistic or that far-fetched for me to decide to move abroad to be a missionary. So my "yes" had enormous implications for them as well.

Seeking Concrete Answers

I wondered, in the days that followed, just what my decision had implied. My routine didn't change, and it left me wondering if I had missed an open door of opportunity that I should have actively pursued, so I sought the Lord on the matter. It wasn't long before I felt an overwhelming need to go on another mission trip. I didn't realize it at the time, but I had made a connection about a year before that would steer me in the right direction.

After the trip to Mexico, I was looking for ways to support my new friends at the orphanage. I wasn't sure how I could donate money internationally until I came across another non-profit, a Christian ministry, in the course of my work. It's fun to see how God orchestrates things, because, of the hundreds of non-profits I was used to working with, one in particular stuck out. I contacted the ministry and learned that its mission was to serve orphans and vulnerable children. After a few conversations with the founder about how to get my contributions to Mexico, I was surprised to find out that part of their ministry was to take donor contributions and send them to Christian partners across the world. And they did it for free. Every single cent I gave would be sent to my friends in Mexico, with no cost whatsoever passed on to them or to me. This was unheard of. I served in a similar capacity at my secular philanthropic job and was accustomed to taking about twenty percent of each donor's gift for processing and overhead costs. Taking a percentage was standard practice. It's how most non-profits kept their doors open, so it wasn't wrong for my employer to do it. I had never heard of anyone *not* doing it.

As promised, one hundred percent of my donation ended up getting to Mexico, and while I was going through my pop quiz, desperate for every prayer warrior to pray me through the test, I had asked this ministry to pray about it. They did. That was not something the leaders of my organization were doing.

So, when the time came that I felt like I should go on another mission trip, I contacted this ministry, because another aspect of their work was to lead mission teams to their partner locations. I was told that a team was headed to Colombia. I didn't know what I was looking for on this new quest, but I had prayed about it long enough to know it felt right, so I signed up.

Defining the Mission

I was given a packet of paperwork to fill out. Included were sections for references and an area to write my personal testimony as a Christian. I appreciated the thoroughness of the vetting process, knowing that a high value was placed on having a quality team of believers who would serve the vulnerable children at the orphanage. This would not be a tourist endeavor.

Another form in the team application packet was one designed to help them appoint an Adventure Buddy. This role was very important to me because I had learned the value of having a spiritual mentor to coach me through life and to challenge me to think. To know what I believed. And *why*. Not to merely believe what I've been told, but to back it up with Scriptural truth. So I knew the Adventure Buddy would be essential in asking pointed questions about what I was learning in Colombia and making sure I didn't miss any pearls of wisdom God had set before me.

Before we left on our trip, the team was asked to attend a series of meetings. In these meetings, we covered things that were never addressed on my first mission trip. We were educated on culture, and what to say, and what *not* to say. Did the Lord anticipate Happy Thanksgiving moments from me, or what? We talked about how the disciples had been called to serve. This was a perfect fit, because God had gotten my attention, and I was trying to figure what it was He was asking me to do. We talked about how Jesus humbled Himself as a model of service and how we wouldn't be arriving as the great white saviors to the poor people of the jungle. And even if I didn't know how to articulate that concept, there had been an aspect of my Mexico mission trip where I thought I'd be going as a hero to those little kids, without ever considering the idea that they would teach me so much more than I taught them. God was already at work in Colombia. We would be joining Him there in the work He was already doing.

We also talked a great deal about how our American culture places a high value on our professional status or what it is we do. It's how we are identified. When meeting someone for the first time, one of the first questions we ask is, "What do you do?" The coordinators emphasized that Jesus wasn't as interested in what we do; He was more interested in who we are. Who we would be. They jokingly told us that Jesus had given us the "Be-attitudes" in Matthew 5, not the "Do-attitudes." Therefore, the emphasis of our mission wouldn't be constructing a building. Truthfully, that could be accomplished by locals for far fewer dollars than it would take to send a team there, and it could probably be accomplished with far better talent than any mission team could provide. I've seen the way high schoolers slap paint on a wall and mix concrete. I know I'm not a skilled electrician or bricklayer, and if I were the one helping, they'd get what they paid for if I came to do those things.

The emphasis was on *being*. We would go to these children from broken circumstances, and we would spend time with them. We had no agenda other than bringing them the love of Christ. We would be His hands and feet.

Tim Dearborn, the author of the short-term mission workbook we studied prior to departure, offered profound insight when he wrote, "In this treasure hunt of grace, our encouragement and affirmation of people may be our most significant ministry." That was music to my heart, because it was spot-on truth that I had discovered firsthand through my pop quiz. It was my turn to give back.

In addition to giving my time and encouragement, I was awakened to another way I could give back — an unconventional way, I thought. As we kept tabs on our fundraising efforts to cover our airfare, lodging, and other costs, a few fellow team members and I were talking about our progress. My default, as with the Mexico fundraising, was to raise a little and then write a check for the rest. I had been saving up for this moment, so I was prepared to do so. But after stating my intentions, my teammate candidly said with a smile, "But why would you rob anyone who could be a part of this blessing?"

Those words struck me. I had never thought about it that way before. Some people enjoyed giving generously, and it was a blessing for them to be a part of our team. Some of them couldn't travel internationally, and their donation would be their way to participate in the work God was doing. So I stifled my pride and took fundraising more seriously, allowing people opportunities to join the mission through financial giving. To accomplish this goal, I decided to have a fundraising dinner at my home which, although the floor plan didn't resemble that of the Biltmore, did have a nice open layout and plenty of room to accommodate a large crowd. I was anxious to fill it full of people.

But to understand my level of excitement over the party, one must first understand the ambitious mission I had made a priority over a series of summers. It was a mission in action, each time a generous bonus came my way, to build a multi-tiered deck down the otherwise useless wooded slope of my backyard. Sweet Daddy. He showed up every weekend with a truck full of tools to help me build this beast. I enjoyed woodworking and learned a lot from him. I enjoyed, even more, the time we spent together and our laughter over construction mishaps and projects that flopped. Many times we scratched our heads, especially when trying to mathematically figure out how to cut a string of stairs down a bizarre slope. It was like Elly May trying to help Jethro Bodine on *The Beverly Hillbillies* cipher his "times and gozintas."

Daddy teased me about always wanting to build things in the heat of a humid, Mississippi summer, and he wondered why I couldn't ever start a project in the winter so he wouldn't have to sweat so much. He began to call our two-man crew Death Valley Construction.

We ended up building a beautiful, three-level deck. The first section attached to the house and had a pergola extending over an outside grilling area and serving bar. A large, ten-foot-long bench sat opposite, and the back of the bench folded forward to make half a picnic table, providing more eating or serving space if needed. That piece was his idea, so he really couldn't tease me about my frivolous ideas or threaten to ban me from the home improvement books at Home Depot.

The middle deck had beautiful, metal spindle railing. It was the perfect place for a table and umbrella, and from it ran several flights of stairs below. At the bottom of the stairs was a flat boardwalk, Mom's idea, which led to the final deck, which was further down in the woods and lined with bench seats.

I couldn't just stop without a finishing touch. My deck needed lights. So, after receiving some pointers and having a smarter brain than mine do the proper calculations, I ran electrical wire and hung fixtures on each level of the deck so it could be enjoyed at night too. Again, I'm no electrician, and I got what I paid for. I prayed I wouldn't zap myself while wiring it and that my house wouldn't burn down once I finished. Luckily, neither happened.

When we finished, Daddy laughed and wanted me to swear, in blood, that I'd never sell the house because we had so much sweat and labor wrapped up in the deck. I had never fully used the space. So my inner planner thought that having a bunch of people over was a fantastic idea and would validate all the labor that "Death Valley Construction" had put into the project.

A few special friends helped me organize the fundraising dinner, and they had mad skills that would put Martha Stewart to shame. Incredible cooks. Incredible decorators. Incredibly in charge. I couldn't have had the event catered any better if I'd called in a professional. Little white tables and chairs and candle centerpieces sprinkled the open spaces on all three decks. It was almost as exciting as having a wedding reception.

About 65 friends came to dinner that night, and kids filled the yard with excitement as they chased each other all over the place. Fabulous food filled our bellies, and I had an open floor to tell everyone what was going on in my life and the mission God was calling me towards. I told them about the children in Colombia and my desire to go see them.

As always, my friends, a fantastic fellowship of believers, generously met my needs. More than enough money was raised to cover my trip costs, and we were able to use the excess to meet someone else's costs. God provided, and we were blessed. I was excited at how God was opening doors in response to my yes. It was total affirmation that I was doing what He wanted me to.

Of course, a few friends didn't offer their full support, or much at all, for that matter. One called me expletive-stupid for wanting to go to one of the drug capitals of the world for some other people's kids and leave my special-needs daughter at home. I knew this friend, and the heart behind the crass sentiment was really one of love and concern, because I was a single mom, and there was always a risk of something bad happening.

But as far as my daughter was concerned, I knew I'd be leaving her in loving, capable hands, and she had always been one of the few things in my life that I didn't lie awake worrying over. I had given her to the Lord a long time ago, and I knew God would take care of her. If He saw fit that my time on this earth should end, then I knew she would be okay. That didn't mean I attempted things recklessly or foolishly, which might have been this friend's perception, but I was trying to live by faith. I was trying to pursue that which I was called to do. I stuck to my guns and offered these explanations, and I reminded everyone that if I could see the future —see it or touch it — then it wouldn't be called faith. And God was calling me to a life of *faith*, obediently following Him, one step at a time.

That was probably the crassest rebuke that I know about.

Other responses struck me too, but I had a strong hesitation about responding directly to them. I thought that, for some responses, like "I could never go to a foreign country," it would be best to live by quiet example and simply let the Lord speak to them in His own time about their personal journey with Him and their level of commitment. The last thing I wanted to do was come across as condemning, or worse, end up resurrecting a dead Pharisee.

Nevertheless, I love to share a quote that is fitting for those types of responses, words that have been hugely instrumental in my perception of missions. Hudson Taylor was a missionary to China, and many of the words he left behind convict us to self-examination. He said, "It will not do to say that you have no special call to go to China. With these facts before you, and with the command of the Lord Jesus to go and preach the gospel to every creature, you need rather to ascertain whether you have a special call to stay at home."

I was on mission. And I was getting ready to go.

Famous Last Words

I remember talking to a friend on the phone one evening as I picked up a few items from the grocery store. I vividly recall saying that I wanted to do what my new friends at the ministry did every single day. I was walking past the end-cap of an aisle, and it displayed Reese's peanut butter cups, one of my favorite little treats, when I made this statement. I didn't realize how sweet that moment would become for me, without partaking of the chocolate and peanut butter delight.

A few days later, during one of our last team meetings prior to departure, I was asked to stay behind to talk. It caught me off-guard. My mind reeled and I scrambled to think of any Happy Thanksgiving gaffes I had blurted out during our time together. I was anxious.

After the meeting, the mission team leader said, "I want you to work for me." There was a long, pregnant pause, because instantly in my heart I knew this was part of God's yes-moment plan for me, and a door had swung wide open. I also remembered that I had confessed a couple of nights before, next to the Reese's peanut butter cups, wanting to do that very thing.

I chose not to reveal what had been going on in my quiet time with the Lord. I was still trying to process it all. This would be a major change for me. My heart was screaming, "Yes!" but my mouth didn't move. Somehow, there was no connection between the two parts of my body.

And then the team leader added one more detail — a tiny little detail, "But I don't have any money to pay you." I'm sure the cheery anticipation on my face dropped like a lead balloon when I heard that. *"Well that's a problem,"* I thought. *"I'm a single mom with a mortgage. How's that going to work?"*

The leader went on to tell me how I would be responsible for raising my own personal support, to pay my salary. I had never done that before, and the only other fundraising efforts I had experienced were largely group efforts by an awesome network of friends. But this was different. This wouldn't be a one-time gift for a one-time trip. I would be asking someone to pay my salary. And that frightened me.

I'm sure the leader saw the look of panic that crossed my face. So it was explained to me why it had to be that way, why that staffing model was chosen. The key reason was directly related to the one hundred percent pass-through feature I had appreciated so much when I used their ministry to send funds to Mexico. In order to keep the ministry overhead below five percent (which is unheard of in the non-profit world), all staff was asked to raise their own support — essentially, to volunteer— so that salary costs didn't affect the ministry's budget or its one hundred percent pass-through feature, and all funds raised for the ministry could be used to keep the doors open and fulfill its mission.

Equally important, many overseas missionaries who served at-risk children used this ministry to receive their personal financial support. They had to raise their own funds; that was how they got their paychecks. Not many agencies were available to manage donors for them and send them one, neat, lump-sum payment at the end of the month, especially for free. And since I had only a teensy taste of how difficult it could be to raise funds, I appreciated the next comment. Missionaries who visited the office when they were stateside would share their burdens from the field, some of which included the financial aspect of fundraising, because it's hard. "We want you to be able to look them in the eye and say, 'I understand.'"

It's true. I had already learned I couldn't relate or connect with someone on a personal level during a trial and say, "I understand," if I had not truly walked a mile in their shoes. I learned this from the pop quiz, as other people with pop quizzes of their own began to clutter my path. God was already using my experience for a bigger purpose, and there was enormous credibility when talking with someone when I could say, "I understand," and actually mean it. I knew that listening and responding would become part of my ministry, part of being real. It sounded so fantastic and my heart embraced all of it, but the actual fundraising part paralyzed me. So much that I never responded to the offer. I was told to go to Colombia, think about it, and let them know after I got home.

And that's where we left it.

CHAPTER 11:

TOOLS FOR DISCOVERY & DISCUSSION

1. Can you describe a time when the Lord persistently pursued
    you for a commitment to Him, for your "yes"? What would a
    full commitment imply for your life? How would your desires,
    choices, and use of your talents change?

2. Have you ever considered going on a mission trip? What do
    you think about the idea of affirming others simply through who
    we are rather than what we go to do for them?

3. Have you been mocked or criticized for stepping out in faith?
    How did that make you feel?

4. What has been your experience when you were struggling and
    the person you confided in responded with, "I understand" and
    you knew they meant it? Do you believe the struggles we've
    faced are intended to be used to encourage others?

CHAPTER 11: A SEARCH FOR BIBLICAL TRUTH
SUFFERINGS AND COMFORT

In chapter 7, we talked about the importance of doing the good works set before us, but what if the circumstances surrounding our good works involve much suffering? We are told in 1 Peter 4:19 to commit our souls to God in doing good. This verse reveals a difficult concept to grasp, especially if you are one in the middle of your suffering. Sometimes our suffering is according to whose will? Why would God will us to suffer? Look back to our study in chapter 10 and recall that God will never leave or forsake us. Also recall that we bear His image and were created for His glory. As incomprehensible as it may seem, Christians are called to glorify God even in our sufferings. 1 Peter 4:16 reiterates this concept. However, 1 Peter 5:6-10 assures us God will strengthen and exalt us in due time. It will always be in His perfect time, not ours. Verse 7 of this passage commands us to cast our cares upon Him, and this directive, yet again, stresses His desire for relationship with us. Why is He looking for us to bring Him our heavy burdens? Because He cares for us.

Now read 2 Corinthians 1:3-7 for further insight about the purpose of our sufferings. According to verses 3 and 4, who comforts us in all our tribulation? He comforts so we can do what in return? Our trials teach us how to relate to others better and comfort them in a way that brings God the most glory. Who is within your circle of influence experiencing trials similar to the ones you've already endured? How can you walk alongside them and comfort them in their grief?

CHAPTER 12

A Pearl of Wisdom

I stared out the small window and the world beneath me looked like a blanket of broccoli tops for as far as I could see. We had already departed Bogotà, the capital of Colombia, and for about four hours we saw nothing but jungle as we flew to a little town called Leticia at the southernmost tip of the country.

Someone commented that this would be an awful place for our plane to go down, that no one would ever find us. To which I replied, "Not me. I've got a knife and a lighter. I'd burn this place down so they'd see the smoke signals and know where to find me." You can take a girl out of Mississippi, but you can't take the Mississippi — the redneck —out of the girl, apparently.

Leticia was unique because it was bordered by the Amazon River, the jungles of Peru, and the city of Tabatinga, Brazil. The two cities, Leticia and Tabatinga, comprised one fairly large pocket of people in the middle of nowhere. These jungle cities were literally landlocked by the jungle with the Amazon River serving as their western boundaries, and the only way in or out was by plane or by boat.

Thankfully, we didn't travel all the way down the Amazon by boat and encounter endless amounts of creepy-crawlies; rather, we flew into the airport in Leticia. The commercial jet we took out of Bogotà, a gigantic city, was about like landing Barbie's jumbo jet on The Little Pet Shop's runway. (Can you tell I have a daughter?) It felt way out of proportion, and I hoped the pilot, George of the Jungle, knew what he was doing, because I was trying hard not to holler, "Watch out for that tree!" That man needed a raise, because he landed us in a tight spot with a few feet to spare. We exited the plane, on the runway, not at a terminal, and we headed for the little shed-like airport to get our passports stamped. Surprisingly, there was a baggage carousel spitting out our bags, but the team of hounds sprinting across it and stopping at each bag with a keen sniffer let me know that Dorothy was not in Kansas anymore. And I recalled the crass comment my friend had made about it being a drug capital and thought to myself, "Well, that explains the dogs." I was thankful that those German Shepherds didn't hike a leg on my bag (which had happened to one of my friends), and I was thankful that the apple-scented hand sanitizer that caught the dog's attention and got me pulled over didn't cause much of a delay. By this time, I had learned to discreetly pack my undies in a mesh pocket because I understood the high probability that my bag would be ransacked and it would be less embarrassing than having them thrown all over the place.

Once our passports were stamped, we were allowed access into all three countries, because they knew it would be impossible to get very far beyond the cities. One could freely walk across a border with no inspection whatsoever and leave Spanish-speaking Colombia for the strikingly distinct Portuguese culture of Brazil. Different language. Different food. Different buildings. Or one could take a boat across the Amazon into Peru and stand amazed at the vast wilderness before them.

Although the two cities hugged each other, the transition from one to the other was surreal, almost like Dorothy walking out of her old farmhouse and entering Munchkin Land. Within a matter of feet, everything was noticeably different.

There were lots of people in these two cities because, over time, the population had grown faster than the infrastructure had expanded. I was told that building roads was almost impossible. By the time that workers had completed the final phase of a road project, the jungle would have reclaimed the earlier portions of the job. And since it was extravagantly expensive to import a vehicle down the long, winding Amazon, most people rode motorbikes. It was common to see a whole family riding one bike, kids and babies hanging off everywhere, with no helmets. And they weren't interested in giving pedestrians the right of way, so you'd best be looking both ways before stepping into the road.

We settled into our rooms at the quaint, comfortable inn. There were no air-conditioners to fight the massively thick humidity that permeated the air. I come from the land of humidity, but this place took it to the next level. Ladies, don't even bother packing a straightening iron, because if your hair is anything like mine, it's going to grow like a Chia Pet® and there's no taming it. We'd be better off going bear hunting with a switch. Wrap up the madness or embrace its bigness, one of the two. The screens on the large open windows kept a breeze flowing through the inn, so getting rest wasn't nearly as bad as I had feared. More worrisome were the lizards scurrying up and down our walls. But I claimed my space, primarily the bed, and said that as long as they stayed in their space, we'd be just fine.

I had learned to lower the bar of expectation on mission trips in terms of accommodations, and to be flexibly prepared for the worst. Just lay that bar right there on the ground and everything would be dandy. Anything could happen. And contrary to many beliefs, these mission trips were not exotic, luxury vacations.

However, the next morning we were in for a pleasant surprise. This is when I met Paula, pronounced differently in Español than in Inglés. I'm telling you, she not only resembled Paula Deen, her American counterpart, but she could cook like her, too. She had a full spread of crepes and fresh fruit and a mass of trimmings to pile on top of it. And this is where I experienced fresh, full-bodied Colombian coffee to the nth degree, poured straight out of a ceramic carafe into my own little cup —a coffee drinker's delight.

For those who didn't want coffee, there was an equally delightful treat in store. Paula squeezed the freshest, homemade juices. I don't know what they were, but she served them with a girly little flower hanging over the rim of each glass, and I had to have one of those, too. Paula was my new best friend; it didn't matter that I couldn't talk with her, because a smile went a long way. She kept the coffee coming. She served us under the thatch-roofed *maloka*, a Colombian version of an open pavilion, in the center of the inn. We would not be scrapping over beans and tortillas this trip.

And just as we had the socks charmed off of us with Paula's delightful quaintness, we met her husband Roberto. Pot-bellied and with no shirt, he was friendly, cordial, and unashamed, and I just smiled thinking of how the attraction of opposites is not confined to any particular culture.

Once we indulged in Paula's treats and had pot-bellies of our own, we began our morning devotion time before we went to see the children we were so eager to meet. We were asked to read quietly. As soon as each of us was entranced in thought and pondering what we had read, our team leader quietly delivered a bundle of notes and cards to each of us. Not a word was spoken, but, one by one, most of us began to sniffle as we recognized familiar handwriting on each inspirational card.

Little did I know, this was the critical role of the Adventure Buddy who had previously been assigned in our team meetings. Letters from family and friends had been collected secretly, and each morning as I received a bundle of five or six letters, my loved ones offered words of encouragement and affirmation and told me how the testimony God had already given me had spoken so powerfully to them. It humbled me; all of a sudden I felt so far from home, but so incredibly loved. Receiving these letters became the highlight of my morning. It's amazing what words of affirmation can do for one — the power of words.

We finally arrived at the orphanage. The property was surrounded by a tall concrete wall, providing protection for the children, and the entrance was blocked by a large, red, steel gate. One pound of a fist on the gate echoed throughout the property, and we could hear a stampede of children running to see who was about to visit.

Smiling, brown faces with shiny, black hair ran to meet us with hugs. Eighty-five children would rotate in and out of the enclosure throughout the day, as the older ones attended school during the first half of the day and the younger ones attended during the second half. In between tutoring and devotions, we would simply play with them.

I had learned a valuable lesson since Mexico, and the picture of the precious little girl standing at the screen door begging for our attention left a lasting impression. I did not want to repeat that mistake and let the busyness of *doing* interfere with the blessing of *being*. I was thankful I didn't have any VBS crafts to assemble and was free from any agenda.

We played "football" with them, a game better known in the States as "soccer." Those kids can play fiercely, and I was outmatched by the tiniest of them. But we had great laughs, a language of its own that transcends all language barriers. We also played basketball and took turns passing the digital camera around so they could capture their goofy faces and laugh at each other. Another thing I learned in Mexico: don't take your most expensive camera.

One of my favorite memories took place in a tropical tree resembling a magnolia, and it provided excellent shade. Platforms had been built throughout the large, twisted branches, and it made a fun space to gather with the kids. Although the girls would play soccer and basketball with us, they weren't nearly as passionate about it as the boys. So my favorite experience with the girls was not only the affectionate hugs, but getting salon treatment on a tree house platform. They clustered around me, aged anywhere from five to fifteen, and began to fix up my hair. Bless their hearts, they had their work cut out for them. They braided and re-braided and tucked flowers into my hair, and once they had me all "purtied-up," we took pictures together. I don't know if my paid-for blonde hair being strikingly different from their own dark hair is what fascinated them most. But it warmed my heart as I quietly let them do their thing. They actually did far better with it than I had done, so I kept the braids. We posed with sunglasses; and they were all smiles and hugs. I ate it up.

Kids came to the orphanage for a variety of reasons. Many of them who stayed there were not true orphans with no surviving parents; they were considered social orphans, or children at risk. Their families either couldn't or wouldn't care for them. Some were rescued from abusive situations. Some came for tutoring or after-school care. And about twenty-five of them lived there permanently, never returning to where they had originally come from.

Many of the kids came from a village on the outskirts of town. It was a place of poverty and an area where the government had displaced a number of families. They lived next to the jungle, and their shanty-town community was a row of wooden shacks that literally sat on the border of Brazil. There was no indoor plumbing, and I was told that the small, muddy pond next to the community is where they washed their clothes and themselves.

We were strictly advised not to gawk at them or take pictures, as if they were on showcase, but the images of how they lived stayed with me and made me feel like I had a castle at home. All those Scriptures that talk about the rich? Yeah. Outside of the States, and in comparison to the billions of people on this planet, we really do live in the elite upper percentage. And most North Americans don't even realize it.

Over time, our team leader and the director of the orphanage established a relationship with the pastor of the primitive village, and he knew we were coming for a visit. I was most excited about getting to worship with another people group, because I knew how much it had meant to me in Mexico. It was simple. No instruments. No building. Just a makeshift *maloka* in the jungle with a dirt floor and a few wooden benches. No deep theology. Just basic truths for a relatively uneducated crowd.

After going to Mexico, I had really made an effort to learn the language. Again, I was kicking myself for wasting my time in school with German. But I got some books and attended a few classes at a local church that really boosted my vocabulary. I spoke like a two-year-old, and was nowhere near conversational, but it was better than nothing, and it was light years ahead of the dirt Pictionary games I had played in Mexico.

I found an old Indian lady sitting in the corner of the *maloka*, and I sat next to her. I wanted to know her story. The deep brown lines in her face told me she had one. She had soft brown eyes, and we did our best to talk to each other as it began to pour down rain. I hadn't experienced rain until I experienced *tropical* rain. In some ways, this old lady reminded me of my grandmother with her quiet strength. I'm sure she had it as the years had not always been kind. Live long enough and that's bound to be a reality. I had already found that out for myself. I didn't learn her story, but it was a pleasure meeting her anyway.

We had been told what to expect prior to our visit and that many of the villagers did what they could to provide for their families. Some were craftsmen and made intricate carvings from wood they collected in the jungle, and they used berries, also from the jungle, to give some of their pieces color. Others made jewelry. This was the perfect opportunity not only to buy souvenirs for our families but also to give them business so they could support their families. We were told that sometimes there would be days in between their meals. That some of the children at the orphanage who went home for a weekend visit with their families might not eat until they returned. We knew food was scarce for them.

One of the most touching experiences of my life happened there in the village right after the church service. We were served by them. They joyfully brought out bags of bread and made some sort of coffee-looking concoction, and they wanted to give it to us. I couldn't believe they wanted to share with us out of their poverty. I was so accustomed to the reverse, to sharing out of my abundance. Their generosity touched me. Deeply.

If I had been Catholic, this would have been the moment where I made the sign of the cross. Catholic or not, this is definitely where I silently blessed whatever was about to be served in dishes that had never seen a dishwasher or, possibly, even dish liquid.

I knew God would bless them for their act of generosity. And it was my responsibility to receive it humbly with grace and consume whatever they dished out, not to be a snootie-patootie and turn up my nose at the unfamiliar. The last thing I wanted to do was offend them by rejecting this gift they gave so freely. I also knew God would bless me too, and cure whatever parasite might be lurking in that unfamiliar food. Thank you, Lord, for honoring that faith and allowing me not to get sick.

However, I must not have had the same humble attitude and prayer a day or so later when we walked through the fish market down by the river. Let me say this: I do not have a weak stomach. My daughter had severe Poltergeist-like reflux and could target you across the room. I spent years reading the looks on her face and catching the blows, especially when we were eating in public. So I was used to all sorts of nasty bodily fluids being thrown at me, and I could practically eat a sandwich with one hand while performing "clean-up on aisle two" with the other.

But the fish market. It was one of two times in my life when I had the seasick, pale white face, symptoms of nausea. I don't know how or why, but it got to me. I'm sure the large, exotic fish being pulled straight out of the river and chopped in a smoking-hot building had something to do with it even though I'm a country gal who's cleaned plenty of fish.

After the casual tour of the aquatic butcher shop, we went to eat across the border in Brazil. The cuisine was different from Paula's fantastic fare, and taking into consideration the onset of something violent, I stuck to plain rice and *carne asada*. The Brazilian food probably got an unfair review that day, but I declared I didn't care to have it again.

We played with the kids as much as we could, and we wanted to treat them to something special. I was humbled, yet again, to learn that many of these kids, who had lived by the Amazon all of their lives, had never been out on the river. There's no way we could have taken all of them on an outing, but, under the director's guidance, a select few were chosen to take a chartered boat with us up the river.

Many of the local villagers used long, slender canoes to fish from, and I didn't know what to expect at first. I wasn't sure if I'd have to Pocahontas-paddle my way around in a river that makes the Mississippi look like a tiny trickle, a river that contains strange things like pink dolphins, piranhas, and other things with teeth much bigger than mine. And I have terrible balance, so one can imagine where my mind was going with the prospect of being in a wobbly canoe. Thankfully, we were able to charter a large passenger boat that carried us up the river quickly and safely.

Somebody asked me if I wanted to jump out for a swim. Heck, no. I'd seen too many movies that showed how fast a piranha could whittle somebody down to a nub, and my luck has never served me well. I quickly passed on that. And I noticed that nobody else was willing to jump either.

We finally arrived at our remote destination, Monkey Island. No, the local jungle folk weren't so uneducated that they couldn't figure out how to capitalize on a tourist attraction. And you guessed it. The attraction was monkeys. Once upon a time, these tiny little monkeys, weighing only about a pound, were brought to this island in the Amazon. Some speculated that they were spider monkeys, but I have no idea what they really were. They were tiny, and they had bright white faces and other incredible features. They could spot a banana a mile away. You'd better be ready when you pulled out the bait, because the treetops came alive like *Planet of the Apes* and, before you could brace yourself, the little ninjas were on your head and everywhere else scrapping for a bite.

I quickly learned to smile with my mouth closed because monkey tail doesn't taste that great. They pounced from head to head and close to twenty monkeys could hang off of one person with outstretched arms, if they were willing to sit still long enough. It was a sight to see. Mommas with tee-tiny babies on their backs joined the crowd. It was feeding time. And what comes right after any good feeding? Yep, monkey poo.

Unfortunately, a team member forever caught my facial expression on camera the second I glanced at the purplish looking jam that oozed down my biceps. Except that it *wasn't* purple jam. There was no need to explain the words that instinctively exploded in my head, because the picture said it all...unfiltered. I honestly don't remember what I thought, but I'm sure it resembled whatever was on my arm. Yes, I am a natural-born sinner, and a work in progress.

The monkeys were fun and a whole new experience, but nothing compares to the little pearls of wisdom God sets before sinners like me. Little nuggets of treasure He allows us to find. And I found one in Colombia.

As I got to know the director of the orphanage better, I realized she was a true gem. The way she mothered almost a hundred children and counseled their families was amazing. Walking with her down the streets of Leticia, one could tell that she was well-known. Locals practically saluted her as she went by. I quickly understood why. She was the Mother Teresa of the Amazon, and she became a treasure to me too.

She and I had time to talk one-on-one as we walked to dinner. She asked me my story and I shared some of the things I had been through. I did *not* tell her about the offer at the ministry that lay on the table.

I had been asked to go on this trip and bring home some pearls of wisdom for my peers. So I kept my eyes peeled all week long. My senses were heightened, and I had seen wonderful things as well as sad things. I was blessed by the entire experience, but nothing particularly significant stood out to me. I hadn't had an "Angelica moment" as I had in Mexico, although we followed the same pattern of emotions and wept when we told the kids *chao* (good-bye). It's never easy to leave behind a child in tears. I don't care how calloused one might be. It'll get to the best of them.

But it wasn't until it was time to leave for the airport that my pearl was revealed. Mother Teresa of the Amazon finally shared her story with me. It was another one-on-one conversation I wouldn't forget.

Our stories had strong parallels. She told me that she had once lived in Bogotá and had a good-paying job. She told me that she had a family that didn't turn out the way she thought it would. And she told me that she accepted the calling on her life to follow Jesus, enter the ministry, and move to the Amazon, where she loved on these little kids. And to top it off, she told me how wonderful it had been serving Jesus and that she wouldn't trade it for anything. No looking back. No regrets.

I felt more connected with her after I knew she had walked in my shoes through similar trials. There is enormous credibility when someone can tell you, "I understand," and you know they mean it. I knew she meant it, and as we talked I realized God was using her as another mouthpiece in my life, to affirm what had been stirring in my heart. I felt the pearl of wisdom I sought forming in that shell of an airport. Everything in my heart seemed to be posted on a script before her as she verbalized my thoughts. Not only were our stories so much alike in a scary way, but she also anticipated the fears I was having about answering the call to give up my lucrative position and enter the ministry. Then she grabbed my hands, looked me in the eyes, and said, "Just say, 'yes, Lord'." There it was. A shiny pearl of wisdom and the perfect affirmation needed to make a significant career move in my life.

Those two little words that had permeated my thoughts since I was caught in a fig leaf and bubbles probably meant nothing to the rest of the world. But to me they meant everything. They were an undeniable confirmation from the Lord.

CHAPTER 12:

TOOLS FOR DISCOVERY & DISCUSSION

1. Do you think Americans, in general, are an elite percentage and rich in comparison to the rest of the world's population? Have you ever classified yourself as "rich" particularly when reading Scripture?

2. Would you say that your generosity towards others has been characterized by giving out of poverty or abundance? How does this question challenge you?

3. What are your pearls of wisdom (defining moments or spiritual markers)?

CHAPTER 12: A SEARCH FOR BIBLICAL TRUTH

CHEERFUL GIVING

In the passage Mark 12:41-44, the Jewish widow contributed all that she had. How did Jesus respond? Now read 2 Corinthians 9:6-15. What does verse 6 say about sowing and reaping? Read verse 7 of this passage closely and consider the widow who gave two mites (the smallest Jewish coins, perhaps equivalent to two pennies today). Is God more concerned with the value you give or your heart behind the gift? What will He make sure we have in verse 8? And in verse 10, what does God do? He is the One who supplies and multiplies. If fear paralyzes or hinders your charitable giving, do you trust the reassurance from this passage that you won't need for anything? In verse 13, who gets glory for our liberal giving? Time and time again, we are reminded of the purpose for which we were created (Isaiah 43:7).

CHAPTER 13

The Philip Syndrome

A Stinky Reunion

The welcome wagon met me at the airport when I arrived home. My parents and my daughter were a sight for sore eyes, except I had a surprising reaction from them when I got into the car. No one but my ever-faithful mother wanted to hug me, and I got the pinched-nose candid response from my daughter, who said that I smelled like a monkey. I'm not sure which part of the monkey she was referring to, but I got the point.

The humidity had been so thick in Leticia that nothing ever dried. Clothes stayed damp, especially my bath towel, and the jungle smell permeated the contents of my bag. I had even soaked and scrubbed in the modern shower when we got to Bogotá. I took my time relishing the unending hot water, which was drastically different from the military showers with cold rain-barrel water that we had taken all week in Leticia. One would think the cold water would feel nice in the humid heat, but I insisted that it was doubly shocking. Despite the modern shower, I somehow still reeked.

My momma was a hairstylist, so another teensy factor in my standoffish welcome may have included my casual mention of children with nits and my asking her to pick up a delousing kit at the beauty supply store. The kid in question may or may not have actually had lice. I don't have the best trained eye for that. But, even if the child did have them, I didn't care. I had learned a valuable lesson about perception with Angelica and her sticky lollipop, and I didn't want to repeat the same mistake and hold back on my love and hugs. I decided if it was true, I'd take care of whatever bugs I picked up once I got home.

Processing the Nuggets

I had gone to Colombia with better cultural training than I'd had when I went to Mexico. So I was prepared for the emotional letdown once I got home. We had been living highly aware of our surroundings all week long, and re-entering our culture would give us culture shock even though it was our native culture. It would probably take several days to pull ourselves out from under the covers to resume a normal routine, and even longer to examine the spiritual nuggets of treasure picked up from our trip. It was also most likely that whoever was holding down the fort while we were gone would be ready to dump it back into our laps. Time to retreat under the covers and mull things over might not be available. Tried. Tested. True.

Most people didn't want intricate details of my trip. They primarily wanted to know that I arrived home safely and had a good time. Another lesson learned. Tried. Tested. True.

But it was interesting to see who did have lots of questions about my trip and who was willing to dig deeper to find out all that God had shown me. It was not the people I would have predicted, but it allowed newer relationships to be formed. For those with questions,

I embraced intimate conversations and shared exciting details, and for those who were satisfied with the one-liner about me having a good trip, I just left it at that.

I still wrestled with the apathy that seemed to pervade our culture of excess. More personally, I wrestled with the mansion occupied by one and a half in comparison to the shanties in the jungle.

None of these irritants dissipated, but my normal routine did resume, and I knew I couldn't change an entire culture. The only person I would be directly responsible for in front of the Great Throne would be me. And I had a question that required an answer. I needed to decide what to do about going into ministry.

Addressing the Question

I knew in my heart, without question, what that decision would be. But my professional training and black-and-white logic defied my heart's response. My head violently opposed my heart, and I began to feel that my choice of profession was a curse, because it flew in the face of faith and challenged every step I attempted to make. Pondering the decision to go into ministry made me realize that. And the pesky thought of fundraising held me back — that casual declaration that there was no money to pay me.

I didn't even like selling Girl Scout cookies when I was a kid. I might have sold two or three boxes, and that was to my immediate family, who probably felt sorry for me. Worse, I hated the fundraisers my daughter brought home from school. The school's attempts to raise money ranged from selling unusually large buckets of popcorn, to cookie dough, to discounted coupon books, you name it, they tried to sell it. And the hook that set my hatred was the fact that if I didn't make the effort to tote her all over town and sell at least ten or more (it felt like a hundred) of the unnecessary items, then she would be penalized for it by having to sit in the library while her peers enjoyed pizza and a moon bounce to celebrate their parents' sales.

I loathed the concept of my daughter being punished for my lack of effort and quickly tagged the idea as being straight from the devil. I wished they'd just tell me how much they wanted every parent to contribute for a new computer or whatever else was going to help my child learn. Sign me up for that. I'd willingly pay the $25 or more for a direct contribution towards a need in lieu of having to work my tail off to burden people I know into paying excessive amounts so that her school might end up with the same $25 once they covered their costs. But, hey, that's just the accountant speaking.

Speaking of accounting, a set of interesting circumstances was brewing at my current job. Dynamics had changed; top leadership had changed; board involvement had changed, and while I had loved working there for the past six years, it no longer felt like a family environment to me. It felt more like the corporate job I had before. I could feel the door closing in the time since the other one had opened. It became more difficult to stay, not only from a professional perspective, but emotionally and spiritually, too.

Remember how we often go through a test after learning something new? I was about to have another kind of test. I was a mouse, and the bait was the big cheese, throwing all kinds of attractive aromas my way and luring me in. I was approached by human resources about taking one of the top leadership positions. The salary would most likely be double what I was already making, and things weren't too shabby for me to begin with. Crossing over into the six digit range got my attention. Oh, the lure, the temptation, for someone who already had an inherent desire to chase a dollar. God was stripping away the materialism, but it was not completely gone by any stretch of the imagination.

I thought about the future, about how I would provide for my daughter in the years ahead. "This could be my ticket to security," I thought. Single-mom. Mortgage. A more reliable vehicle. That would only happen when the wheels fell off my 4-Runner, of course, because I still clung to the promise of recouping savings and not having a car note as long as I could, since my unfortunate mistake of not negotiating its price.

I knew deep down I'd kick myself for taking the bait of the big cheese and not going into ministry. It'd be like taking the easy way out instead. My accounting brain compared the options. On the left hand, I saw zero dollars available, and on the right hand, I saw mega dollars. I was confused. I'd always heard the old saying, "If it looks like a rat, and it smells like a rat, then it's probably a rat." This is how it felt, but I wanted to be sure. Again, logic attempted to dominate faith, to search for an explanation, to settle for a black-and-white answer.

So I sought counsel with trusted advisors, and it was brought to my attention, with laughter, that only God would provide the answer to the test before He allowed it to be given. What did that mean? The abstract answer only frustrated me more. I wanted somebody to tell me what to do. And, just like when I was pregnant with my daughter, no one would utter a word as to what I should do. So I laid all my nuggets of treasure out on the table and thought about them, long and hard.

Part of this assessment included thinking back to how a previous crossroad had demanded a decision. I recognized that abortion might have been the easy way out in some people's eyes, but, thankfully, I submitted to the fact that God would take care of me and my daughter. And it had been proven. We both had been well taken care of. We hadn't missed any meals. I hadn't missed paying any bills. God provided. Tried. Tested. True.

Why would this particular crossroad be any different? Why should I opt for the easy way out? I knew that God had been tapping me on the shoulder and trying to get my attention for quite some time. I knew I didn't manufacture all the "Yes, Lord" moments. They were real. How could I not factor that into my decision? Why was I struggling with this decision so much?

The answer came to me in another quiet evening hour, just as it did when I was reading the passage in John about Jesus asking Peter if he loved Him. This time, I was reading about Jesus feeding the five thousand. Each of the gospels gives an account, but John gave me some information that I hadn't considered before.

The disciples had just received news that John the Baptist, Jesus's cousin, had been beheaded, and Jesus wanted to go to a private place to rest for a while. Many people had seen and heard of His miracles and wanted to get a closer look, so they followed Him. And in no time, a multitude of people surrounded Him. It was late in the day, in a desert, mountain area. Jesus was not annoyed by crowds following Him. He was moved with compassion because they needed a shepherd. They needed Him, whether they recognized it or not. Perhaps many were there to just see another miracle, not to hear a sermon, but Jesus met their deepest needs and chose to teach them about the kingdom of God.

After a while, the disciples wanted to send the people away to neighboring villages so they could buy some food, but Jesus didn't want them to go away. Instead, He told the disciples to give them something to eat. In response, the disciples asked Jesus if they should spend two hundred denarii to go and buy food for all the people.

Was it a rhetorical question? It was certainly a quick mental calculation of what it'd take to feed all those people. A single denarius was equivalent to a day's wages, so they basically asked if they should go buy bread using about eight months of wages to feed the five thousand men. If the women and children had been counted too, then it could have been closer to twenty thousand people needing to eat. I don't carry eight months of wages in my pocket, and I'm sure they didn't either. Maybe all they carried was pocket lint, just like me.

Now we get to pick on Philip. Philip was one of Jesus' disciples, and I am so glad we have a record of his floundering, just like we do of Peter's. Misery loves company, perhaps, or maybe it's just a relief that Philip was a black-and-white kind of person like me. What we find out next is recorded only in the gospel of John.

"Then Jesus lifted up His eyes, and seeing a great multitude coming toward Him, He said to Philip, 'Where shall we buy bread, that these may eat?' But this He said to test him, for He Himself knew what He would do. Philip answered Him, 'Two hundred denarii worth of bread is not sufficient for them, that every one of them may have a little.'"
John 6:5–7

Jesus intentionally gave Philip a test. As for my test, the mouse and cheese demonstration, the answer I was searching for was readily available in the account of Philip and his lack of faith. I just had to see it more clearly.

Like me, Philip probably put on his little green banker's visor, whipped up an Excel spreadsheet, summed up all the estimated expenses, and, with a big sigh, declared in absolute confidence, "It can't be done."

If we wanted to make this more dramatic, Philip could have inserted another column into his spreadsheet. We don't know for sure, but let's throw out a possibility. If we back up a verse, we learn that the Jewish feast of Passover was approaching. It is possible that bread supplies disappeared during Passover, just as they do with the mere threat of snow in Mississippi. The storm doesn't even have to happen, just the threat of it. And the bread vanishes.

But Passover wasn't a forecast. It was an appointed day set by God. There was no question when this feast would occur, so it is possible that many were getting prepared, and the local bakery wouldn't have enough to accommodate the masses even if they did scrape up the two hundred denarii. I love it when a plot thickens — drama — which only fueled Philip's doubt. Philip was resolved. It cannot be done.

But it *was* done, even though there were only five barley loaves, two small fish, and a bunch of pocket lint instead of denarii. Jesus' miracle of feeding the masses was just as much for Philip's benefit as it was for the rest of the crowd. And He put it in Scripture for my benefit too. Jesus is patient, even when our belief isn't where it needs to be. We don't start out being super-Christians, but He knows that, and He knows how He is going to help us to grow.

I continue picking on Philip, because he was a slow learner like me. If we fast forward to a point after Jesus miraculously fed all these people, we see that Philip *still* showed weak faith. And I can't help but wonder if Peter was relieved to know that he wasn't the only disciple to stick his foot in his mouth?

> "Philip said to Him, 'Lord, show us the Father, and it is sufficient for us. Jesus said to Him, 'Have I been with you so long, and yet you have not known Me, Philip? He who has seen Me has seen the Father; so how can you say, 'Show us the Father?' Do you not believe that I am in the Father, and the Father in Me? The words that I speak to you I do not speak on My own authority; but the Father who dwells in Me does the works. Believe Me that I am in the Father and the Father in Me, or else believe Me for the sake of the works themselves.'" John 14:8–11

Philip still wanted visual nuggets of truth. It simply boils down to this: "Show me," Philip asks, "and it'll be sufficient." Oh, Philip. Would he still need visual proof before he would believe? He had already seen Jesus' miracles. He had heard Jesus teach about the kingdom of God. He stood face to face with Jesus, but he wasn't making the connection.

When Philip asked to see visual proof of the Father, he was completely missing the deity of Jesus as one of the three distinct persons of the Trinity: God the Father, God the Son, and God the Holy Spirit. Jesus is God's Son. He has all the powers of God in Heaven. There was ample proof. Healings and miracles, one after the other, tangible proofs, evidences, and fingerprints of the Holy One right before Philip's eyes, and his finite mind still couldn't comprehend all that he had encountered. Silly Philip, silly me.

I was Philip to a "T." As I read this passage, I realized I had been missing the point, too. I literally had a spreadsheet worked up at the office and saved on my desktop. I had crunched the numbers just like Philip. I had my budget laid out, and without ever uttering the words, I had convinced myself, "It can't be done." Convicted. And guilty as charged.

I wanted to go to the ministry, but the fundraising part had paralyzed me into not making a decision. And even though I procrastinated and sought adequate denarii to provide my security and my meals, Jesus patiently showed me that He is the big cheese, the One who will provide. So I surrendered this decision to Him and once again, said "Yes, Lord." I now knew what had been so funny when I had asked for advice. It was apparent to everyone but me, apparently. I just had to learn for myself, through faith. I simply needed to trust what He was calling me to do. That He would provide even if I didn't see it laid before me yet. I didn't realize that my "Yes, Lord" would apply to so much, including the decision to trust Him with fundraising and finances.

Finally, being resolved in heart and mind, I went to work with a smile. I told my friends who had wanted me to jump at the job opportunity that I had good news, and I had bad news for them. I always liked to start with the bad news so I could end on a softer note of good news. I told them the bad news was that I wouldn't be their boss. And the good news was that I was leaving the company. At least it was good news for me.

The encouraging part of Philip's story is that it didn't end with broken faith. Jesus patiently grew him, and in the book of Acts we read how Philip was instrumental in building the early church. There was hope for Philip. There was hope for me. And there is certainly hope for you. Just like the loaves and fishes, there is no shortage that Jesus can't supply. It can be done. Just remember that when all you see is pocket lint.

CHAPTER 13:

TOOLS FOR DISCOVERY & DISCUSSION

1. Has your faith ever been tested and you declared, "It can't be done?" Have you simply asked for the Lord to just "show you"?

2. How has God responded to your times of weak faith? Can you draw a line back to extra measures of grace shown in order to help you grow?

CHAPTER 13: A SEARCH FOR BIBLICAL TRUTH

LIVING IN FAITH DURING THE WAIT

Hebrews 11:1-3 describes what faith is. The faith "hall of fame" is narrated in subsequent verses. Read Hebrews 11:4-12:2. According to verse 6, what is required to please God? What does He reward? In 12:1, we are called to run our race with what? Who do we look to (Hebrews 12:2) for help in running with endurance and faith?

The book of Habakkuk also reinforces the importance of faith especially while we are waiting on an answer from God. Recall our discussion from chapter 11 about God's perfect timing. In Habakkuk 1:2 we see the prophet Habakkuk overwhelmed and impatient with his struggle until he finally cried out to God, "How long?" (I prefer to hit the fast-forward button in my struggles too!) What was God's response in verse 5? He told Habakkuk to look, watch, and be astounded. We know from Isaiah 55:8-9 that God is infinitely bigger than our human brains can comprehend. He basically tells Habakkuk this in Habakkuk 1:5 pointing out that he wouldn't understand the reason for the wait if God literally showed him. Nevertheless, God reassures the prophet in Habakkuk 2:3 to continue waiting for the appointed time. How does God tell him to live in Habakkuk 2:4 (especially during the wait)? How do we live by faith? Read Habakkuk 3:17-19. Even if all the things we hope for don't come true, we are to find joy in the God of our salvation as He gives us strength in all that we do. That's how we live by faith. Remember our salvation alone is reason enough to rejoice while we wait on other things to come to pass.

CHAPTER 14

Roadways in the Wilderness

Private Petitions

New chapters were being written in my life, and I had a heart change about certain things I was praying for — and not praying for. One of them was about new beginnings. God was redirecting my career and giving me a new beginning there, so why not in my personal life as well?

I had sworn I'd never get married again. Famous last words, and I should have learned by that point never to say, "never." Because "never" rarely panned out according to my plans. But then again, I should also have learned that my plans were essentially futile, because God had much bigger and more purposeful plans for me. And He's the One in control anyhow.

Despite the fact that I was sticking to my guns about staying single, some of my friends still amused me with their matchmaking proposals. One potential setup was with a recently divorced pastor, who had five kids. No, thank you. I had been nervous enough about having one kid; no telling what kind of wreck I'd be with a house full of six curtain-climbers when the two families meshed.

Another matchmaking proposal that tickled the fire out of me came from a friend who had a brother I'd never met. The brother was my age and had never been married. Red flag! At my age, everybody had some kind of a past, so I pegged him right off the bat as having something wrong with him. I mean, why hadn't a woman already scooped him up if he was so wonderful?

I had my heels dug in. I had a rejection ready for any proposal headed my way, and I wasn't the least bit interested in starting over. My life had reached a peacefulness that I appreciated.

Nevertheless, I came to realize I'd had a bad attitude about starting over with someone new, and I eventually began to pray that God would place a special someone in my path. I certainly wasn't going looking for him and would rather have been beaten with a cane pole than to have to go through the dating process again, especially in my season of life. So I had another Philip moment and just asked the Lord to plop him right in front of me: make him cross my path and show me.

These prayers occurred about the same time I was preparing to go to Colombia, a time when I still hadn't received clarity about my "Yes, Lord," and was open to whatever He had in store for me, even if it meant putting my heart out on the line again.

God heard my prayers and gave my attitude an about-face. I had a new, cheery anticipation. It was wildly exciting, but terrifying at the same time. I never told anyone about my prayer. It stayed between me and the Lord.

Sugar Plums

I had volunteered to teach children's Awana at church; this little club helped the kids learn God's word by memorizing verses in a fun way. My friend and I taught the kindergarteners. We divided our class into two smaller groups so we could get to know each of the kids better and have time to hear their memory verses. My daughter was in the first grade group because I had learned from the previous year that she would listen to another teacher better than she would me. I opted to stay at the kindergarten level and let her advance to someone else. She needed different experiences with different teachers, so it was a good fit.

Kindergarteners are so naïve and sweet, and I enjoyed spending my time planting seeds with them, especially during the large group time when they'd fight over who got to sit in my lap. I only had two arms, so space was limited. I think I accommodated three at some points: one in each arm and another nestled in the "criss-cross apple-sauce" chair of my lap.

I remember telling my friend at work, during our tea time break, about my new group of kids in Awana. I told her about this one little boy in particular who had caught my attention. He was quiet and had a smile that melted my heart. There was something different about him, enough that I would single him out and tell my friend about him. It was a uniqueness I couldn't quite put my finger on, but I told her that he had the face of an angel. I realized, after the first Awana meeting, that I had met this boy's dad about a year before through a church outreach event where we went in groups to connect with people who had visited our church. So not only had I met him once before, but I had also been to his house with several of my friends during the visitation hour.

As the dad approached me in the church gym that first night of Awana to deliver the appropriate security tag to pick up his son, he instantly recognized me and called me by name, or something very close to my name. I was impressed he got it that close. He was friendly, and we smiled as we recalled our prior meeting.

One of my responsibilities as an Awana leader was to reach out to the children each week. Obviously, a kindergartener wouldn't have his own phone and contact information, so I had to draw from the parent's information on a roster in my leader's book.

I left this little boy a voicemail on his dad's phone to give him some cheery encouragement for the week. Another time, I reached out to him through his dad's Facebook account, which required me "friending" Dad first. I didn't think much about the contacts I made, but they did force me out of my comfort zone to contact the parents and get to know them in order to reach the children. I began to get nervous about drafting a note to this one student, because it required going through Dad. God gifted me with two eyes and, even though I'm blind as a bat without my contacts (with them I have near perfect vision), I noticed that Dad was good-looking. And Dad began responding to my notes as I attempted to reach his son. His friendliness was just as hard to ignore.

One of the conclusions I drew about Dad in my initial assessments was that he loved his son enough to have him at church every Wednesday night. That told me that it was important to him that his child be grounded in faith. The other conclusion I drew about Dad was that he had a past, too, because I never saw Mom during drop-off or pickup. Her name was on the roster sheet, but I had never met her. So I reasoned there was something to it.

It didn't take long to discover that Dad had gone through a pop quiz like mine, because in one of his responses to my attempts to reach his son, he told me that his son spent half the week at his mom's house and half the week at his. Boom. There it was. Confirmation that I wasn't crazy, and my intuition was correct.

Being a divorced single parent, Dad was the one to ensure that his son was there on Wednesday nights. I respected that about him. Deeply. Because in all my church-going years I had noticed that many women were the ones dragging their children to church. So it stood out to me that this man would bring his child faithfully, without any prompting from a woman. Based on what I had observed, I felt it was somewhat rare.

The other thing that I respected about this man was the fact that he knew what it was like to be a single parent. It gave him credibility in my eyes, because he was walking in my shoes. That was actually one of the things I had prayed for in a new partner. I didn't pray for the single, never-been-married type, because I knew there'd never be any way that someone like that could relate to me in the truest sense.

The Awana year coincided with the school year, so for a couple of months I exchanged pleasantries with this man as he brought his son to church. Rarely did they miss, and I found out it was only when my student, or his older brother, was sick that they'd stay at home. I had never met the older brother, but that wouldn't be the case for long. I already knew there was a different family dynamic, because a second child in my Awana class had the same unusual last name. My friend and I tried to make the connection by asking the two boys if they were cousins, because they looked nothing alike. They smiled and told us that the one in my friend's group was an uncle to my little fella. I could not figure out how that worked for two kids the same age, and I probably looked like the nostalgic RCA dog when I cocked my head to one side in puzzlement. The kids knew it and thought it was funny. I knew there was another kid around there somewhere with the same last name. I just hadn't met him yet. This was the brother that I had been told about.

As the months passed, I found myself keeping it quick and simple, because Dad intimidated me. I'd wrap his kid in a jacket and direct him out the door to his father, something like, "Here. Here's your kid." Like so many other situations before, my heart, mind, and body weren't always on the same page. I knew what I had prayed, but crossing that bridge and putting things into action would be a different story. Bottom line, I was scared to death. My Colombia trip had come and gone; December was around the corner, and Christmas was rapidly approaching.

One Wednesday night during the Awana large group session, I was approached by a boy who declared that his daddy wanted to go out with me. And just as fast as he had run up to me and blurted out this shocking confession, he disappeared. I never saw his nametag, and was left thinking, "Huh?" I didn't make the connection, nor did I think much more about it, because this one man had caught my interest and my eye. I just wasn't willing to admit it to anyone yet, not even myself. But it was true.

A few weeks elapsed, and I realized that the colder months were harder on my little fella because of his asthma. He had missed some classes because of his struggle with it, and I missed seeing him. I also noticed that Wednesday nights weren't filled with as much anticipation without the two-second pleasantries with Dad at drop-off and pick-up. When he returned to class and his asthma was better, he decided to open up and talk with me a little more. Normally, he was quiet as a church mouse. But he revealed a piece of information that put all the pieces of the puzzle together for me.

He told me that his daddy wanted to ask me if we would like to go look at Christmas lights with them. Visions of the boy approaching me like a bolt of lightning a few weeks before flashed through my mind, and instantly I realized, "Ahhh, so that was your brother." Now, I had two statements of Daddy's intentions, and it was clear he had been talking to his boys about me. Panic, like you wouldn't believe!

I knew class would soon end; Daddy would be picking up his little fella, and I hadn't had time to process the mystery I had just unlocked. My only recourse was to avoid an embarrassing Happy Thanksgiving moment by gathering every crayon and crumb I could find as soon as class ended. I even felt the need to reorganize the supply cabinet as eyes in the back of my head looked for Daddy to come and go.

I left my friend hanging to single-handedly deal with all the kids, papers, coats, and parents that night as I grabbed a broom and swept every corner with my back to the door. I was in a corner, literally, and I had no idea what to do with myself.

I had a couple of days to think about the upcoming proposition, and I learned how to compose myself after the initial shock of it all. I still had to make weekly contacts with my kids, so when it was time to reach out to my little fella, I sat at my work computer and struggled to find words. How was I going to reach out through Daddy and pretend as if neither boy had approached me? Surely they had told Daddy what they'd done, and most likely they'd snickered when they did. I figured he intentionally had them break the ice, because he was probably scared to death, too. Why not use the kids to do our dirty work, right? I was glad the ice had been broken, because I like to brace myself for what's coming, just as I did when I found out about my daughter's spina bifida. These situations weren't even close in comparison, but I still liked to be ready, not caught off guard and grasping for a grip on my composure.

I sent the message, and the response brought the question I had braced myself for. It was casual. Not obnoxious. Very down to earth. It included my daughter, and since we were a dual package, I appreciated that. This man didn't know it, but I loved Christmas, and one of my favorite traditions had been looking at Christmas lights. My daddy use to gather us up on a cold winter night and drive all over the country to find pockets of people who bothered stringing lights. Red lights were my favorite, and ever since my childhood, I've felt like a big kid when going to look at lights. I liked his unique invitation, and I appreciated that it wasn't the clichéd dinner and movie where there was enormous pressure to keep a conversation flowing in order to avoid awkward silence. So, having Christmas lights as a conversation piece was actually an ingenious idea.

Men, take note. The idea was fun, light-hearted, down-to-earth, wouldn't break the budget, and didn't have an ounce of pretension to it. I wasn't interested in showy muscle cars or jacked-up trucks, or anything else that would be a haughty show masking the true identity of the one behind it all. I had already seen his quaint home and his vehicle, and I didn't detect any of the pretense that I had come to loathe from many in our culture. He seemed real. And that was attractive.

The more I thought about it, the more I loved the idea of going to look at Christmas lights with him. And after I had run down the office hallway to a friend's office to squeal and freak out and share all of this with her, I came back to my computer and calmly crafted a response. Of course, my friend wanted to get the scoop and see a picture of him, so Facebook accommodated, and her excitement only added fuel to my fire. She was the only one I had told about my new crush.

Our messaging back and forth was a great opportunity to clear the air on obvious things prior to meeting, mainly discussing available times to see the lights when we both had our children. We agreed to meet about a week later, which gave ample time for my nerves to do their thing. Without a doubt, I was excited about our date, but I was concerned about taking my daughter along and having his kids there, too. I needed to know how much I liked him before throwing our kids into the mix, not that his boys weren't already aware of the upcoming event. This was a whole new ballgame for me. And I didn't know the rules.

He did call me before our date so we could talk privately without a class full of kids making silly faces at us. The first time I saw his number appear on my phone, I am sure I paced a path in my kitchen as I walked back and forth trying not to let my anxiety reveal itself in my voice. It was daylight when he called, and we talked until the last bit of light faded into darkness. I know this because I was peering off into the woods outside my kitchen windows the entire time I paced and soaked up the conversation, and when we hung up I suddenly realized that I was standing in darkness. I had not even turned on the porch lights.

Again, I like to see things coming my way, so since I chose not to put blinds on the windows on the back of my house facing the forest, I made it a habit to keep the back porch lights on. My reasoning was that if something was going to come and get me, at least I'd see it coming and could have weapons ready. It was my way of dealing with fears and living alone.

After I turned the porch lights on, my house shone like a beacon in the forest, and I realized a new light of joy had entered my life, a beacon of hope. After our long conversation on the phone, I realized that I wanted to see him before the scheduled date. I didn't want to wait a week. I wanted to talk to him with no kids, and I wanted to get to know him face to face. I wrestled with how to approach him about it without coming across as desperate or even skeptical.

Finding balance had always been a challenge for me, and I was worried I'd say the wrong thing, but I ended up sending a casual text message asking if he'd consider meeting me for lunch one day prior to looking at lights. He accepted, and I was even more excited that I had two dates lined up, and I'd get to visit with him sooner than expected. I kept telling myself that I wanted to get to know him better, but the truth was that I already liked what I saw. The few things I knew about him were enough to know that it all lined up with things I had prayed about.

Now, the challenge for me was keeping my private excitement just that, private. Because the last thing I wanted was a billion questions from a billion different people as they watched my life unfold like a soap opera. I didn't want any outside influence manipulating my emotions. I wanted it to be pure.

I had already bluntly declared to my friends that I wasn't interested in dating, especially any old men in a shoe with so many kids that I wouldn't know what to do. I also didn't want them getting the impression that I had entered the dating world again and was ready to book my calendar with all their perfect candidates.

This was different. And even though I had just booked two dates with my mysterious man, I didn't see it as testing the waters. My prayers had told me this wasn't happenstance. I was enjoying the nugget of treasure God had placed in my path without any interference from curious friends and family. I wanted this moment for myself, so I chose to keep it private until I felt ready to reveal the exciting news and deal with all the publicity.

That was the challenge to having lunch. Thankfully, my daughter begged to go home with my parents like clockwork every Sunday afternoon, so I banked on that habit when we scheduled lunch after church. There weren't many times my predictions were accurate, but I knew my daughter, and she didn't disappoint. And because of her predictability, I didn't have to go public about what I'd be doing that afternoon.

We met at a restaurant, and just as we'd had on the phone, we had the best conversation. Our visit lasted for several hours, and it settled any question in my mind. He was definitely worth pursuing, and I was even more excited about seeing the lights with him and our kids.

Date night finally came, and I had racked my brain for hours on what kind of treats to get his kids for the enchanted excursion. A simple Snickers wouldn't do, so I asked around and finally found a bakery that made the cutest decorated cookies. I wanted this to be a special treat, so I bought a box for the kids, because I was actually making an impression on three fellas, not just one. They say great minds think alike — well, he had also brought treats for our kids to enjoy on our night out. We met at the church parking lot, piled into his vehicle, and drove through the city's Christmas light displays. It felt good having the five of us together, and I enjoyed my time with them. It just didn't last long enough.

After what seemed like a lightning-quick light show, we headed back to the parking lot where I had left my car. The kids got out and ran off their sugar-high in the lighted parking lot. I had never seen my little fella so lively. They all seemed to be getting along well, and it gave me another chance to have one-on-one time talking with my man.

The air was cold, and when it began to bite, he offered me his coat so he could stand there and freeze instead of me. We talked for a while, and it was time to get our young kids in bed, so he gave me a warm good-bye hug — and, boy, did he smell good! Did I have to let him go?

I was sold. Everything about our new relationship felt so natural and right. He was everything I wanted. We burned up the phone lines from that moment on, and I can't explain how remarkable it was to learn that after hours of conversation with me even late into the night, a time would come when he would politely end the conversation, because he had a bigger conversation that needed to take place. He would tell me, "It's time to go and spend some time with Jesus." We had talked much about spiritual things since our first phone conversation, and this was without a doubt the key to my heart. He loved Jesus just like I did.

I had a saying taped to my computer at work to serve as an ever-present reminder for me to choose wisely. I posted it when my prayers had changed and before I met my new love. The statement, written by Max Lucado, reads, "A woman's heart should be so hidden in Christ that a man should have to seek Him first to find her." Everything this man did, he did right.

Christmas Eve night, it snowed; my daughter was at her dad's, and there was a magical sense about the night. I felt like a kid again, and as we talked on the phone, my urge to see him was irresistible. So I put my 4-Runner in four-wheel drive and drove a couple of towns away to see him. He would have done the same, but his vehicle didn't have four-wheel drive, and I insisted this was a safer choice. We sat and talked the entire night away, nonstop, and I studied everything about him down to the faint little freckles that peppered his face. If ever there were a moment in time I wanted to bottle, that would be it. My heart pounded, and butterflies filled my stomach, and I knew with absolute certainty he was the one. God had crossed my path with this beautiful person and literally showed him to me, just as I'd asked Him to.

It was a magical time in the midst of a winter wonderland. It was a Christmas unlike any other, and I recognized 'twas my night before Christmas that presented an unexpectedly special gift. I cherished the moment, and I laid snug in my bed with visions of sugar plums, and my perfect man, dancing in my head.

New Things Springing Forth

One of the things our team was asked to do prior to going to Colombia was to write a personal letter to Jesus about the things we hoped to learn from our experiences there. I had forgotten about this letter by the time my new romance started.

It was a cool afternoon, and I was spending some time of my own with Jesus. I remember sitting on an ottoman I had scooted up so that it was inches away from the fireplace. It was warm, and I was reading in Isaiah, one of my favorite books.

The mail carrier came by and dropped some envelopes into my box, so I ventured out to get them and resumed my place by the fire. A letter with a hand-written address caught my attention. "That's odd! That's *my* handwriting," I thought. I had forgotten all about addressing an envelope too, but I'm sure our mission team leader kept the assignment ambiguous enough that it was easy to forget. He never told us what he'd be doing with our letters to Jesus, just as he never told us the role of the Adventure Buddy and the fantastic letters we would receive in a foreign country.

I opened my envelope, and there was my letter. It was untouched; our team leader had clearly never laid eyes on it. Over a month had passed since our time in Colombia, and it was fascinating to read my thoughts, fears, and prayers prior to embarking on that journey. I opened myself up to more "yeses" in God's treasure hunt. Tears streamed down my face as it became evident how much God had done in such a short period of time. He was blessing the socks off me for my yes, and seeing how perfectly He was knitting the new threads of my life together left me speechless.

After reading my letter and weeping with joy over God's miracles, I resumed my reading in Isaiah. The verse before me perfectly summed up this milestone in my life. In the very same chapter where God promised that the rivers wouldn't overflow me and the fires wouldn't scorch me, I found a new promise.

> "Do not remember the former things, nor consider the
> things of old. Behold, I will do a new thing, now it shall
> spring forth; shall you not know it? I will even make a road

in the wilderness and rivers in the desert."
Isaiah 43:18–19

I knew the true context of that chapter in Isaiah was Israel's redemption and the Redeemer, but it sure had personal application for my life as well.

The letter I had written talked about letting go of former things and making peace with them. And when I did, my new love sprang forth, not only for Jesus but for my new man as well. I recalled the advice I had been given about God not taking me out into a desert, flipping me a quarter, and telling me to call someone who cared. I had been through some hard times, and God showed me there was a road out of the wilderness: His road. And right then, it was as sweet as could be, like the road in Candyland, minus the pitfalls, lined with candy canes, gum drops, and sugar plums — and it all danced in my head.

CHAPTER 14:

TOOLS FOR DISCOVERY & DISCUSSION

1. Have you ever had to make a new start? If so, what were your fears?

2. What roadways in the wilderness has God prepared for you?

CHAPTER 14: A SEARCH FOR BIBLICAL TRUTH

FEAR AND GOD'S HOLINESS

Fear can be paralyzing. The Scriptures are full of verses and admonishments to not fear. However, fear has a proper place. We learned from King Solomon in our chapter one study that the only place for fear is fear of the Lord (Ecclesiastes 12:13). Solomon also wrote in Proverbs 1:7 that fear is the beginning of knowledge. What did Jesus teach in Luke 12:4-7? Which of God's powers are expressed in verse 5? Didn't God Himself teach His children to fear Him in Leviticus 25:17-18? Aside from the fact that He told us to, why fear God? Leviticus 11:44 and 20:26 gives us the answer. God is holy. God's holiness cannot be in the presence of sin. This simple fact amplifies the significance of Jesus being our high priest and mediator reconciling us to Holy God through His perfect blood sacrifice (Hebrews 8:1-6).

Moses understood and respected God's holiness and longed to be in His presence. In the passage of Exodus 33:12-23, Moses asked God to be with Israel. God did grant this request, but what was it Moses asked for in verse 18? What was God's response in verse 20? Because we are finite beings, we can't fully comprehend not being able to look at the face of holiness. Isaiah experienced this encounter firsthand in Isaiah 6:1-8. How did the seraphim describe God in verse 3? What was Isaiah's response to being in the presence of the Holy One in verse 5? Isaiah basically said, "I am a dead man." What grace was shown in verse 7? God is mighty, all-powerful, holy, and worthy of our fear, but let us never lose sight of the lavish grace and affection He has shown towards us through Jesus Christ our Lord and Savior.

CHAPTER 15

I Do

Shot by an Arrow

Valentine's Day is one of those holidays that can leave someone floating on cloud nine or digging a tunnel under the covers until the full twenty-four hours has lapsed into history and it's safe to emerge without colorful reminders from every bouquet and helium balloon that you aren't celebrating what everybody else is celebrating. When you do have something to celebrate, it's such a fun day. I've been on both sides of the coin, and I would much rather be one of those people grinning like a possum with all my obnoxious Valentine's Day goodies.

Christmas had passed, and love was in the air just in time for Valentine's Day. I don't think Cupid could have done a better job of showering me with gifts and attention. My new love did Valentine's right. I had never been the recipient of so much attention, ever. He couldn't have scratched his head over deciding what to purchase. He just bought it all. Beautiful tulips, oversized balloons, chocolates, trinkets, and cards. It looked like Cupid sprinkled magic dust all over my house, and I loved it. For months afterward, I found little hard-candy conversation hearts hidden all over my house. He never bothered to tell me if I hadn't found some. He just let me find them in due time, so every day was like an Easter egg hunt. I found them in my freezer, in my clothes drawer, on mirrors, in my car — anywhere I might go and not suspect a sweet little surprise and affirmation of affection. A smile stayed plastered on my face.

We both knew instantly that we were an answer to each other's prayers, and we quickly decided that we wanted to get married. It was not a decision we took lightly; we both agreed that we wanted to do things right this time around. It would be a second marriage for both of us, and both of us had, at one time, declared that we would never get married again.

Specific lessons I had learned from divorce stuck with me. I was aware of old habits that plagued my first marriage. And I didn't want to repeat them. I learned the hard way that a woman couldn't change a man. No one could change another person, for that matter. I learned that it wasn't my job to try to be someone else's Holy Spirit. Only Jesus can cause true heart change in a person.

Another valuable lesson was that anything could be idolized, even a relationship. An idol is anything we seek that takes the place of God, and, in my first marriage, I had placed a man on a pedestal and sought everything from him. It was an unfair expectation for any man to fulfill. It was destined to fail. And it did.

I was aware of many things that didn't work the first time around, things I didn't want to become an issue this second time.

We talked openly about meshing our lives together and getting married for months, but the official proposal came on an Easter weekend. In true gentleman style, he had gone to talk to my dad about marrying me. I had been out on my own for quite some time, but I still thought it was sweet and honorable of him to want my dad's blessing. I didn't know he had approached my parents, and I didn't know my daddy had given him some clues that would put his proposal over the top for me. It was no secret that we had considered ourselves engaged. I didn't have a ring yet, but I didn't care. I had learned that a ring was simply a symbol and didn't secure a commitment of the heart. And I felt secure in his affection for me.

On Good Friday we went to attend a David Platt Secret Church service in Little Rock, Arkansas. It was designed to be a serious, in-depth worship experience, similar to the way Christian churches in Asia were meeting, despite the high stakes of persecution and the threat to their lives. It was an amazing experience that fulfilled my craving for real worship and went beyond cookie-cutter Sunday ritual where often you could find church goers bored to tears and with no enthusiasm, as if they'd rather be someplace else.

However, I had no idea that my new man had a secret of his own. After the Secret Church service, he surprised me with a bouquet of flowers and took me to hike the closest mountain he could find, which was just outside of Little Rock. I had never been to Pinnacle Mountain, but I thought it was beautiful in comparison to the flat lands where we lived. And since he didn't clue me in on his surprise, I hadn't brought appropriate climbing attire. I had on flip-flops, and I thought the big boulder field I was about to climb would be interesting, as those sandals kept sliding out from under my feet on the incline.

Neither of us had hiked Pinnacle before, so we had no idea how far up the summit would be. Once we got to a spot high enough to provide a fantastic panoramic view of everything below, we stopped to catch our breath. Or that's what I thought we were doing. I sat there, engulfed in the beauty of the moment, looking at the skyline, when I heard him ask if I was ready to be his Mrs. And when I whipped my head around, there was a velvety black box displaying more than enough bling to take my breath away. It was perfect. Exactly like the rings I had been eyeing, and I was touched that he had studied me enough to know what would make that moment perfect. For all the things in his life where he had foregone flashy luxuries, this was not one of them. He spared no expense, and it was all for me.

I was speechless. He got me. I had no idea what he had been planning, and it was a perfect surprise. Then we enjoyed a lot of laughs as he told me he didn't realize he had a hole in his jeans pocket where he had placed the ring, and he had panicked several times up the boulder field as he felt it slide down his leg, and worried it would fall into the dark rocky cracks of oblivion. Thankfully, it didn't, because I can only imagine how attractive his soon-to-be bride would look, bottoms up and face down in the cracks digging for another rock. It was a perfect day with my perfect man.

We talked at length about what we wanted and what we didn't want for a wedding. Since I had already been through all the pomp and circumstance of a big wedding, placing a high value on an audience focusing their attention on me, I didn't want that this time. I wanted nothing like it, actually. My life had become simpler, and we wanted our wedding ceremony to reflect the lifestyle we hoped to embrace. We also knew how quickly it could get complicated as we blended our families and decided where to draw the line on an invitation list. To invite one, we would have to invite another, and then another, and before long, it would have snowballed into a three-hundred-plus guest list.

We had met intimately and privately, and that is how we wanted our wedding to be. We considered eloping on a beach and reciting our vows only before God, but we didn't want to rob our parents and children of a blessing, so they were invited to attend our ceremony at the courthouse. I wore a simple, white cotton dress, and he dressed up in slacks. My daughter carried flowers, and his littlest fella carried the ring. It was sweet. Simple. Perfect. Even if he was forty-five minutes late, and the boys had been picked up without shoes, and he had to stop to buy some for them, and the minister wondered if he was going to show. Every great story has drama. I was confident in him and knew he wasn't the best manager of time. I accepted that about him. I also knew that picking up his boys in another town and fighting rush-hour traffic to get back to the courthouse on time would be a challenge. The minister wasn't convinced, though, and we laughed because each of us thought we were right. This time, I was right. I knew my husband.

Taking the Plunge

This time of saying "I do" wasn't confined only to my husband. There was another commitment I needed to take action on. It took a little nudge from my husband to move me to turn in my resignation at the non-profit and accept the position at the ministry. I had made my statement of intent to both the ministry and my other employer, but I essentially kicked and screamed for about seven months before I took the plunge into living off of self-raised financial support. My husband was very instrumental in getting me to make the move.

It was time. The door was closing for me at the other place, and it had become difficult for me to enjoy going to work each day. It was a telltale sign that I didn't need to be there anymore. I recall experiencing a new kind of culture shock in going from the much larger work environment to being one of a three-man crew. Two of us were essentially part-time, not quite working a full forty-hour week. I wasn't handling millions of dollars anymore, and the threshold of what expenditures we had considered "immaterial" at the other job was drastically different at the ministry. Every dollar was handled with utmost care, and even though that should have been the reality at the non-profit, it wasn't. I respected the due diligence at the ministry.

Although the accounting was not difficult, the CEO was deeply relieved that he didn't have to wear that hat anymore, spending late nights and missing out on family time trying to perform bookkeeping which was not his primary skill set. I was actually impressed with how well-organized the ministry had been kept, seeing how thin they had been spread. And I quickly learned I'd be wearing multiple hats too. It's how a small office works. Toilets need cleaning?

Put your hat on, Sister. Floors need sweeping? Get your hat. Mail needs stuffing? We've got a hat for that, too. Part of my culture shock resulted in the transition from a corporate atmosphere to that of a relaxed ministry. From frivolous spending to penny pinching. From wearing only one hat to wearing multiple hats and doing things not confined to my professional skill set.

One of the first encounters I had with office culture shock was during a Christmas card program that we facilitated. We had churches, businesses, and individuals all around town hand-craft individualized Christmas cards for each child at three or four of our international locations. The entire board room was reconfigured with card tables and large, white storage boxes. The boxes were organized by international destination, and as we received large bundles of Christmas cards, we sorted and filed them by child and location. It was fun to see how crafty and creative some people could be.

I recall struggling with sorting the South Korean children's cards, because they all had names in slightly varying forms of Lee, Kim, or Soo. All one hundred of them. And as I stood there trying to decode who was who, I thought to myself, "What am I doing?" I wasn't using my degrees; I was sorting Christmas cards. For a brief moment, I felt like I had slid back down the rungs of that corporate ladder. I knew it would take some time to purge my system of the corporate mindset, and it wouldn't take too long to relax and embrace the work I was doing. So I went back to filing cards. Besides, I enjoyed getting to wear my jeans to work without getting the stink-eye from Human Resources.

Once I regained perspective and grasped the bigger picture, I thought I would have loved to see the kids' faces when FedEx delivered the boxes and they were each handed a folder all of their own, with glittery personalized cards in their native language. What kid doesn't like to receive mail? Most of these kids didn't have sweet grandmas to drop cards in the mail for their birthdays, so I imagine it meant a great deal to them to receive the greetings and words of encouragement.

I didn't get to see their faces firsthand, but we did receive photos of the children smiling with their cards. I knew that photos didn't always capture the fullness of the moment. Go stand on top of a mountain or on the edge of the Grand Canyon with all your senses running on overload, and compare the experience to the pictures once you get home. It's just not the same. But it was rewarding to get even a small glimpse of the fruits of our labor.

A Major Milestone

Life had changed drastically for me. A new chapter was being written.

A new family.

A new ministry.

A new perspective.

Looking back, I had come so far. God had taught me so much. He graciously restored joy and happiness to my life. And it felt like I had arrived to that mythical place I had always longed for: contentment.

CHAPTER 15:

TOOLS FOR DISCOVERY & DISCUSSION

1. Have you ever avoided a holiday because of a past hurt? How did you cope when you didn't want to participate in the festivities?

2. Have you ever tried to change a person? What do you think the Holy Spirit's role is in leading a person to change?

3. Name some idols you've had in your life. Have you ever considered that a spouse or a child could be considered an idol?

CHAPTER 15: A SEARCH FOR BIBLICAL TRUTH

THE ROLE OF THE HOLY SPIRIT

Before Jesus was crucified and resurrected, He promised His followers that the Holy Spirit would come as a helper. Read John 14:15-31 and John 16:5-15. What was promised in John 14:16? How long will the Helper abide with you? What will the Holy Spirit do (read John 14:26)? Not only does the Holy Spirit teach, but what else does He do according to John 16:8? On what authority does the Holy Spirit act? Read John 16:13. Why does He do this (verse 14)? God's promise of the indwelling Holy Spirit is crucial for the believer, because it's through His Spirit that we are taught, convicted, and led to live out His will for our lives.

CHAPTER 16

The Powder Keg

One-Way Tickets to Our Destination

The funny thing about contentment is that it isn't a destination. It isn't a sandy beach with coconut oil and fruity drinks. It's not some place in which one arrives and life is all hunky dory ever after, although it'd be sweet to be able to buy a one-way ticket and never be asked to leave. It's a state of being. And just as one experiences a wide range of emotions on any given day, contentment, likewise, doesn't come with a money-back guarantee. It can come. And it can go.

The truth is that having a blended family is hard. Each player comes to the table with some hefty baggage. And everybody deals with their garbage in different ways. Some like to sweep it under the rug, pretending it doesn't exist, until a mountain appears. Others like to recycle the mess over and over again. I do the latter. With the best of intentions, I try to take a pile, process it, and refine it into something better. More useful. But it's a stinky, laborious process, and sometimes toxins like stubbornness, insecurity, mistrust, or jealousy leach into the family field and poison the environment.

In addition to having dormant emotional scars of divorce come alive like a smelly beast, blended families can deal with parenting complexities. Due to family dynamics and inherent differences, raising children who are subject to multiple outside influences is not easy. All the hard labor of molding an offspring can be unraveled in a single encounter.

Even with these basic challenges, there are still plenty of good times to savor as a blended family, and the reward is all the sweeter when triumphs supersede the adversities that seem to be perpetually stacked against us.

Sweet Reward

One of my favorite memories with my new family was a trip to Silver Dollar City, a theme park in Branson, Missouri. Unfortunately, my husband had to stay home and tend to his HVAC business, which ran full steam in the summer months. So I loaded up the kids and headed for the hills. My stepsons had never experienced the thrill of a roller coaster before, and I was dying to see it through their eyes for the first time. Anticipating the kids' dimpled grins was far better for me as a parent than being on the coaster itself. And I love roller coasters. It was the gift of experience I longed to give them.

When paying admission, I felt like I could have paid for four children's tickets, because being there brought out the child in me. I was bombarded by fond memories of years past when I'd go visit my great-grandmother at her farmhouse in a neighboring town. I was elated when we got to visit Silver Dollar City and see the outdoor play *Shepherd of the Hills*. For me, it was the ultimate experience of the Ozarks as the rowdy Baldknobber gang burned Dad Howitt's

cabin to the ground. That's another cherished story that has reso-
nated with me over time.

As soon as we entered the park, I had to find a map so we could
get our bearings and figure out how we wanted to navigate the maze.
The kids would have preferred to take a shotgun approach because
everything caught their attention. But I preferred to outsmart the
masses and come up with a strategy to tackle the rides.

We could have stayed only five minutes, and it would have been
worth the price of admission just to see the looks on their faces. It
surpassed the excitement of Christmas morning, when packages are
ripped open and, in a matter of minutes, the anticipation is gone.
This was like a treasure hunt with prolonged adventures, and these
were my little pirates.

I could tell after glancing at the map that they all had different
interests. So I gathered my mateys and told them on the front end
that we were going to have a good time. Period. There would be no
fussing, because this was vacation. We were going to laugh and have
a blast. I explained that each of them was different and most likely
would have their own favorite rides. We would do all of them. Probably more than once. We would all have our turn, and when it was
someone else's turn to have their five minutes of fun on their favorite
ride, we would all join in and respectfully accede to fulfilling their
wishes.

I am so glad I put on my eye patch and gave them a stern but loving squint before we embarked on our journey, because we had the
most fantastic time. It was magical how we all got along and yielded
to each other's preferences. The trip really upped the ante for any
future vacations.

Off we went. Three on foot. One on wheels. Since my daughter's
legs were weak, I knew that a full day of walking would be difficult,
so I brought her wheelchair. I could tell that pushing her up and
down those Ozark hills would test my stamina, but the boys were
fantastic and helped out with the responsibility. Sometimes their
legs tired, too, and they hitched a ride on the back of the chair. The

chair was a lifesaver, and it kept us from having to carry backpacks and other goodies.

I learned years ago at Disney that having a handicapped kid was a fast-pass ticket to the front of the line, so waiting became a non-issue. Most people embraced the concept, and cheered us on with red carpet treatment, understanding that it was a noble gesture that momentarily made my little one forget the frustration of the everyday challenges that a handicap can present. Blessings really do come in all shapes and sizes.

Even though Silver Dollar City had its own red carpet program, we somehow timed our trip for a day when there were essentially no lines. I don't know how that happened, but the Lord smiled on us as most of the old folks had left the park by noon and we had the rest of the day to run circles through the rides. It was fantastic.

First on the list of priorities was to experience a roller coaster. I knew the boys had to get it in their blood, because I wanted them to run like maniacs through the rest of the park trying the other ones, too. Thunderation was the first ride we rode. One adult, three kids. As the only adult chaperone, I found it tricky getting lined up in the proper slots so we could stay together. Two of the kids would have to ride in front of me in the two-seater carts while the third would sit next to me. My oldest stepson, who was only ten, seemed the most anxious about the ride. While the other two giggled and jumped up and down, he was quietly reserved. And just before lining up on deck to be next on the ride, he tried to bail on me. "What?" I thought. I put my best coaching skills to the test, because I knew he had talked about wanting to do this for a long time, and I truly felt he'd be missing out if he didn't go through with it. So I encouraged him to please get aboard and give it a try. Yep, he was the odd man out. "You're sitting with me, buddy." I knew I had to keep a close eye on him, because he was scared. I was concerned, but I wasn't going to let it show. I know kids feed off of emotion, so I played it cool. Kept it upbeat. The train pulled up, we jumped in, buckled up, and shot out of the barn.

It didn't take long for this coaster to make a large spiral funneling downward, and the g-force of the circular motion got to him. His face was white as a sheet, and despite the paralyzing power of the spiral, he proclaimed he wanted off. Well, dang, I was in the middle of a moving whirlpool. How could I solve this problem? I lunged towards him, against the g-force, and put both hands on his legs, got in his face, and kept telling him, "It's okay. It's okay."

I was beginning to feel horrible for pushing him into doing something he wasn't comfortable doing. I was ready to take a blow of chunks in the face if that made up for it, because I was sure he was approaching that point, judging from the look on his face. I still didn't know if that'd make up for scaring him, though. My heart sank, and I felt like I was going to be sick for not making a wiser decision.

We looked like a group of Don King wannabe's by the end of the ride. My new hairstyle was simply an added bonus. We looked ridiculous, but I didn't dare laugh until I knew it was safe. So when the train came to a screeching halt in the barn, my stepson didn't move a muscle. He just sat there, expressionless and pale, for a long moment. It felt like an eternity as I waited on his response. He still gripped the bar that had already been released from his lap, and I just knew he probably wanted to slap me or something. But then the most glorious thing happened. He looked at me, grinned, and proclaimed, "Let's do it again!"

With a big sigh I thought, "Delayed reaction there, buddy." I about had a heart attack. It was a tiny hurdle, but we overcame it, and the games were on from that point on. And we did ride Thunderation at least three more times, at his insistence.

We moved on to other roller coasters in the park. He decided he'd more cautiously take a gander at how the other tracks were laid out and at other people's reactions, before hopping back into another line. For example, the Powder Keg exploded straight out of the gate at about 100 miles per hour, or at least it felt like that as everyone's

heads were thrust back into the seat. Nope, he wasn't having anything to do with that one.

Thunderation was his favorite. He had already crossed that
bridge of terror and gotten comfortable with it, so the other extreme
coasters didn't appeal to him at all. I was perfectly content with
his decision. So he would stand safely next to the attendant while I
escorted my other two thrill-seekers on the more adventurous ones.

My daughter had been a thrill-ride junkie in the past, so I
assumed that nothing had changed. I sat her and my youngest
stepson in front of me on the park's newest thriller, called Outlaw.
My oldest stayed safely on the ground and stared up at the vertical
descent we were about to take. He probably thought, "Y'all have lost
your minds."

We took the drop, and my daughter screamed her head off, and
I thought that was normal because she liked to be loud anyways.
Yeah. The doctors said she wouldn't talk, but talk she did, and it was
usually in one volume, loud. After the drop, the track twisted into
a series of upside-down spirals, and then went through some upside-
down loops. It was so fast I literally couldn't see for a second.

When it was over, I was hoping for the same reaction from them
as the first roller coaster ride, but my daughter was livid. She had
been crying, and the force had snapped her ponytail as it whipped
in the wind. Don't mess with a girl's ponytail. She had wanted to
ride, and I accommodated. But she quickly scratched this one off her
re-do list.

Much to my surprise, a little buckaroo was born on the Outlaw. A
thrill-seeker emerged from my youngest fella, and he was electrified
by the experience. I renamed him Wild Bill as he ran circles through
the Outlaw line, but instead of one sweet face next to the attendant,
I now had two. And they smiled in delight with the ground beneath
their feet as they marveled at their fearless sibling.

I got tickled seeing their personalities unfold on these rides. I
thought I had met my match with Wild Bill. Two down, one to go I

thought. Would there be anything in the park that would cause this child to cry uncle? Nope.

I couldn't leave two children standing on the sidelines as I tested the limits of one, so we moved onto less intimidating rides like the Lost River. It was hot, and the kids all loved water. It was the perfect refreshment as the rapids spun us like ring around the rosy, and it was hilarious to see which one of us would take the fall and catch a frigid white-water wave to the back. It was loud, obnoxious fun guessing who was going to get it next.

Emerging as soaked river rats, we decided to go to the larger-than-life Barn Swing to dry off. I was pretty sure they needed clearance from air traffic control to operate this thing. As our feet hung loosely in the air and the hydraulic beast flung us up towards the sun, the nearby Lost River shrank and began to look more like a lost hair. My oldest didn't volunteer for any subsequent swings on this ride, either.

I finally found the one ride they unanimously loved. It was a roller coaster called Fire in the Hole. It was a mild ride that took them indoors through a series of burning buildings, and right at the end of the track, in complete darkness, a bright light and the sound of a train headed straight for us, just as the track plunged, descending into a pool of water that splashed us all. The surprise scared the pants off them, because it was dark and they couldn't see what was coming. It was awesome, and I had more requests to repeat this ride than any other. Hands down, this was their favorite.

In between thrills, I let them play freely in a three-story ball pit while I sat soaking in the sun and watching. Ball cannons lined the pits, and I was amused to see the reactions of their unsuspecting targets as they fired off rounds. Big, little, fat, skinny, young, old — they didn't discriminate. I was just glad I wasn't one of them.

Another one of their favorites was shooting laser guns during a carefree float amongst an indoor maze of a million targets. Raccoons, possums, bandits, explosives ...we shot 'em all. Excitement grew as scores rose and we competed to hit the most targets. It was funny to see who insisted that their gun wasn't aiming right, and whose scores couldn't be correct.

After wearing ourselves out on all the thrilling rides and games, I felt a duty to indulge them with treats they don't normally get at home. Why not sugar them up and let them run more circles through the park? I was seeing dollars well spent and felt like I was getting my money's worth. And I couldn't help but buy a platter with a grilled medley of corn, sausage, and onion. Its aroma is hypnotic and fills the air. The same goes for kettle corn and for the delicious, fluffy funnel cakes fried to perfection and sprinkled with powdered sugar that leave their mark from ear to ear. There are some things you have to buy when you go to a theme park, so go ahead and build it into the budget!

After having treats and beginning to unwind for the day, we took time to meander through the craftsmen's exhibits and marvel at their skills. The most interesting, in my opinion, was the glass-blower who took a rod and some raw materials and shoved them into a fiery furnace that was glowing bright red at thousands of degrees. The craftsman went through a process, and showed the crowd how to make a glass vase. It was fascinating to see him mold a bunch of nothing into something.

Our last stop in the park was the gift shop, which visitors must funnel through in order to exit. Clever design. Once candies and souvenirs were purchased, one could decide if a tour down into Marvel Cave was on their bucket list. I used to love going down into the depths of the enormous cavern as a kid, but my kids didn't seem too interested. I guess the thought of being in a cold, damp, dark hole didn't appeal to them. And they were spent after a full day at the park.

On the way back to the hotel, I decided to drive through Taco Bell and grab some quick dinner. The lady at the window handed us our drinks, and we sat for another minute waiting for the food. In this lull, my oldest decided it would be funny to take his straw and blow a tiny little spit ball at my nose. It stuck, right on the side of my nose, at the exact moment the lady opened the window to hand us our food. The kids howled at my paper wart and thought it was hilarious. I humored them, for the moment, because I was captive behind the wheel with a bag full of food in my hands. But it wouldn't be that way for long.

I gave him full warning that I'd get him back once we got to the room. And I did. I practically hog-tied him, held him down, and licked him in the face. Spit for spit. Sweet revenge. The kids went wild. Sometimes boys beg for rough play, and he got what he asked for.

Particular Parallels

Our trip was a deposit into the family's memory bank, one I'll always treasure. And the more I've thought about it, the more I've realized that our vacation to Silver Dollar City was a great picture of what it's like to have a blended family.

Joining two families under one roof is like stoking the Powder Keg. It starts off fast, and sometimes you have to hold on to your hat. It's a lot of change in a short period of time.

And it can be surprising to learn who wants to sit on the sidelines and not join in on the explosion of changes. It could be a family member. It could be a friend. Some may embrace the new family and consider it a blessing. Some may not, and they draw distinctions between "bloods" and "steps." It's not fair, and it isn't right. But it's a reality. Not all people adapt well to change. But change is, indeed, a given.

Traditions change. Holiday schedules change. There are more extended families to consider, and getting everyone together at the same time, in the same place is almost impossible. Kids revolve in and out, going to each side of their families. And since agreements were made and put in place that everyone shares a predetermined amount of time with the kids, you just have to let them go.

Once the Powder Keg goes off and the family is united physically, it's wise to have realistic expectations and understand that it takes time, most likely years, for a family to bond emotionally.

It would be a great idea to put on a patch, lay out some guidelines for the mateys with a loving squint, and talk about how the crew is going to discover the treasure. But if the crew isn't willing to work together, it's going to take a lot longer to find what they're looking for.

When we married, we were eager to enter the Lost River and willingly jumped into the raft, knowing there'd be rapids. But we didn't know what they'd look like or when and where they'd come. Having a past can create baggage. And scars. And time did tell how my scars would manifest, predominantly through insecurity and fear. The boat did spin. It was only a matter of time until my insecurities spilled over me and left me feeling soaked and cold. But we held on to the safety ropes with each surge until we reached calmer waters.

And as we navigated forward, other ebbs and flows took shape, and sometimes it felt like pushing a wheelchair up and down hilly paths. It was hard. Our handicaps weren't always physical. Many times it was an inability to speak another's love language fluently, effectively addressing matters of the heart, if at all. We discovered a language barrier in our own backyard.

But how rewarding it was when we finally broke through the barrier and hit our targets, as we did on the laser ride. Everybody likes brownie points, right? Using the right words and speaking your spouse's language is worth a lot of points. On the contrary, it's a slippery slope if we choose the wrong words. Negativity can leave us feeling like we're in a cold, dark pit like Marvel Cave. It's best to pass on that experience.

Sometimes it's not a slippery slope, but an instant pitfall that causes us to drop as fast as the track on the Outlaw. Vertically. We've had additional stressors such as two house floods and unending chaos with home renovation. It wore us out. And as soon as we thought we had made it through one drop, another would come our way. Honestly, there were times I just couldn't see for the moment.

Such was the case when I lost my best buddy, Cotton. He stood faithfully by my side for twelve years, through every roller coaster life threw at me. He never failed to greet me at the door. He never criticized my shortcomings. And his last year was incredibly difficult as I dreaded the moment that I would have to make the humane decision to put him down before cancer took its final toll. Wrestling with whether it was the proper time to make the call and coming to terms with the decision I made ripped my heart out, and Cotton's final breath was more than I could bear. It took the wind out of my sails for months. My poor husband did all he could do to cheer me up, but it felt like I was down for the count. John Grogan said it best in his book *Marley & Me*: "A dog has no use for fancy cars, big homes, or designer clothes. A waterlogged stick will do just fine. A dog doesn't care if you're rich or poor, clever or dull, smart or dumb. Give him your heart and he'll give you his. How many people can you say that about? How many people can make you feel rare and pure and special? How many people can make you feel extraordinary?"

Cotton had my heart, and he had given me his. And after he died, I was depressed. Depression took its toll on me, as did other emotions that crept back into my daily routine. As I recycled past hurts, mixing in new ones too, I struggled to forgive. I became bitter, again, and it began to fester. And like the ride Thunderation, a spiral descending track is the only one the train of anger and bitterness follows. It'll make one sick to the stomach and wanting to get off.

Even when the sun broke through the darkness of depression, and the ball pit seemed like a harmless place to be, there were times I realized that I made a wonderfully easy target in the crosshairs of insecurity. Again, hindsight is 20/20. Taking a hit to the face with a big plastic ball may not hurt or ever show a physical mark, but emotionally, one small puff from a cannon and a light tap from an insignificant ball can bring an insecure person down. That's when I had to realize what my weakness had become, put on my big girl panties, and deal with it.

As noble as that sounds, sometimes we don't deal with it properly. And as with the spit wad pasted to my nose, sometimes we want revenge. Whether it's by grabbing cannons of our own and spitefully firing back a few rounds or hog-tying the offender in order to prove a point, neither is productive, and sometimes we just don't do the right thing.

Natural-born sinners. That's what we are. And we must yield to the truth that it isn't all about us. It isn't about getting our way. Or proving a point. Or getting even. It's about giving God honor and glory. And if anything we say or do isn't filtered by that simple truth, then our efforts are vain, and we've missed the entire basis of Christianity.

No matter what challenges we face, I always like to draw a line back to Scripture, our anchor, to know how to conduct ourselves. It will forever be our safety line that tethers us and snatches us out of the snares we've walked right into. We must give preference to one another and behave like Christians, or it's a recipe for destruction.

> "Let love be without hypocrisy. Abhor what is evil. Cling to what is good. Be kindly affectionate to one another with brotherly love, in honor giving preference to one another; not lagging in diligence, fervent in spirit, serving the Lord; rejoicing in hope, patient in tribulation, continuing steadfast in prayer." Romans 12:9–12

That may require dying to self. Daily. Laying down selfish ambition, or personal preference. Remember that love, true agape love, is sacrificial and not self-seeking. I know that's much easier said than done. So don't miss the last part about being patient and steadfast in prayer. God never disappoints. If you don't have it, ask for it!

We start out like coarse sand at the glassblower's shop, and over time and with some high refining temperatures, we become something much more beautiful as the rough edges melt away. But it takes time. And possibly some discomfort.

I'm guilty of being idealistic, and my idealism carried over into my new family. I wanted the Norman Rockwell scene. I wanted family dinners, bedtime stories, hugs, and kisses. Just as I had done before, I longed for things to be a certain way. A traditional, idyllic way.

But I found out that my expectations were very much like putting a square peg into a round hole. It just didn't fit. Not everybody cared for Norman Rockwell, and everyone had different ideas of the picturesque family. So we ended up being less traditional and in tune with something edgier, a little more rock and roll.

I like rock and roll, but it's not what I expected. I've learned that an expectation can be a disappointment waiting to happen. After a while, I realized that we just have to be willing to concede and be flexible. To change our expectations. Not necessarily lower them or give up on them, but to set them with more realistic parameters. Not only when it comes to scheduling, but in dealing with one another as well.

There comes a time when we willingly get on the Barn Swing, let our bare feet hang loosely, toss away the big, heavy shoes we've tried to fill, and regain a better perspective of the rivers that seemed to overflow us. With a ten-thousand foot view, that river doesn't look so big. We begin to see how everything is laid out, and we begin to understand that the one path we've been trying to take leads to nowhere. We let go of trying to plow through a dead end. It's the other path that leads to the concession stand.

And that's where treats are finally dispersed. We begin finding nuggets of affirmation that were years in the making, and we experience love, hugs, and milestones as sweet as fudge.

Through trial and error, blending a family becomes an art of finding a balance that seems to fit everyone, like discovering the ride at Fire in the Hole, where everyone comes out smiling and satisfied. And they're ready for more.

At the end of the day, we may recall the initial sticker shock of entering the park, but the treasures found within, with all the screams, drops, and giggles, were definitely worth the price of admission.

Blending my family has been a roller coaster ride, and I'm so glad my husband is the one still sitting in the cart next to me, by my side through life's twists and turns. Have I wanted to get off the ride of turmoil at times? Yes. Has he wanted to unbuckle my seatbelt on an upside-down loop? Most likely. But we've made it through the explosion of the Powder Keg and the waves of the Lost River; we've climbed out of the darkness of Marvel Cave, held hands through the drops of the Outlaw, and stayed in the cart during the spirals of Thunderation. We've found the path that takes us to the concession stand. And it's such a sweet place to be.

But one must beware. There are seasons when the lines aren't long and absolutely nothing stands in our way of repeating the process. Daily rides in the Barn Swing are necessary to keep a proper perspective. If Jesus isn't the One making our rivers look small and our paths clear, then it's likely to be a scary ride. We must let Him strap us in and tether us to eternal hope, knowing that no maze or obstacle is too great to keep us away from the concession stand. We just have to follow His map to get there.

CHAPTER 16:

TOOLS FOR DISCOVERY & DISCUSSION

1. What insecurities do you carry? How does it poison your relationship with others including the Lord?

2. How has idealism been damaging in your life? How have your expectations negatively influenced your relationships?

CHAPTER 16: A SEARCH FOR BIBLICAL TRUTH

EXPECTATIONS AND DESIRES

Often, we develop certain expectations and project them onto others. But where do these expectations come from? Isn't it fair to say that the desires of our hearts determine the things we pursue, and those desires ultimately influence our ideas and expectations? Shouldn't we tell the truth about our desires and check to see if they align with God's will? Read Psalm 51:6. What does God desire? If we aren't fully aware of the truth about the desires of our hearts, doesn't this verse verify that He will give us the wisdom to know what was once hidden? Doesn't He know our hearts (that He created) better than we do (Psalm 38:9)?

If we have tendencies to elevate ourselves to a high position that only God is worthy of occupying, and if we find ourselves trying to control and change other people instead of letting the Holy Spirit perform that role, then we have found ourselves stepping out of bounds and in need of repentance. We should pray what David prayed in Psalm 51:10 after confessing his adulterous act with Bathsheba. God can and will create a clean heart within us.

Read John 14:13-14 and James 4:1-3. Ask for the right things that honor Him, and He will provide. Whom shall we delight in and desire most (Psalm 37:4)? As noted in our chapter 6 study, Philippians 4:8 is a great reference to sift the substance of our desires. Given the proper desires, we will be able to adjust our expectations.

CHAPTER 17

Somethin' is Brewin'

"Wind's in the east, mist coming in, like somethin' is brewin' and 'bout to begin. Can't put me finger on what lies in store, but I fear what's to happen all happened before." At the beginning of *Mary Poppins,* Bert sensed a change in the wind, something to come.

I sensed something in the air too, and there were reasons our two little families didn't go straight from the Powder Keg to the concession stand when we first joined together. We knew there would be challenges. We just didn't know what they would look like. As time unfolded, those challenges began to take shape.

One of my biggest fears was financial insecurity. The initial sticker shock of the admission price prevented me from fully enjoying the rides, both at the ministry and at home. Raising financial support was difficult for me. Many of the people I thought would support me monthly didn't. In fact, few did.

And it scared the pants off me. I monitored my support account, and when it dwindled, I panicked. I was tempted to go back to fishing, as Peter had done immediately after the crucifixion. But I couldn't do it. Because I knew Jesus had appeared to Peter after the crucifixion, restored him, and commissioned him to a higher calling. And Jesus had met with me, too. That milestone in my spiritual journey remained an anchor for me. And I held onto it.

I also held onto all the other moments that drew me into ministry. None of those were happenstance. I knew I was exactly where the Lord wanted me in terms of ministry, but I had a long way to go in terms of faith. And it was my lack of faith that caused me to flinch with every financial uncertainty. Of course I prayed about these things, but I wasn't praying in faith. I just wanted God to show me a sign, like Philip had wanted. I just wanted a guaranteed, steady paycheck, because in my mind, that equaled security. I never took into consideration that God controlled steady paychecks too. He could cause one to lose a "secure" job, or to be injured in a way that one couldn't work anymore. Any number of things could happen at God's divine hand that might make that guaranteed steady paycheck go "poof."

But I longed for it anyway. I didn't enjoy worrying about a support account with no padding. And I didn't enjoy fundraising, because it felt like I had barked up the same trees so many times that I couldn't keep asking the same people to support me. They all knew what I was doing: that I had gone into ministry and was raising financial support. And for whatever reason, most of them didn't step forward to support me. Perhaps they all assumed that someone else would step forward to foot the bill. I was at the bottom of the barrel. I had exhausted all of my contacts, and I didn't know who else to ask to support me.

The plot thickened, as it did when Philip scratched his head over how to feed the five thousand, and not only did he see an insufficient support account, but he also saw limited supplies at the bakeries. He most likely felt there wasn't much to fall back on. No safety net. No cushion.

This was how I felt, because I wanted my safety net to be my husband and his line of work. But he was self-employed, and like most who have ventured down that path, there are seasons. One may be feast, and one may be famine. The cycle goes up and down like the roller coaster. There are lots of unexpected twists, turns, and drama in owning your own business. And the uncertainty of it all unsettled me. And I lost count of how many times I just prayed for him to have a regular eight-to-five job, because it was that steady paycheck that was going to give me peace of mind.

You see, I was still in a trap, a snare, one that I had never recognized before on my journey. Of all the traps I had hopped into and been set loose from, this was the one I blindly dragged around the longest. I started out chasing a dollar, and even though God had grown me in many areas, this one area still needed attention. God used my husband in many powerful ways to show me the trap I was caught in. But instead of listening and yielding to what was being said, I bristled, beat my chest, and fought back.

All those verses about money didn't seem to apply to me. I knew God was dealing with my desires about bigger, fancier things, so I had a faulty impression that I had "arrived" and that money was no longer an issue for me. Until the steady paycheck disappeared.

As we fought over money and I spewed my poisonous darts, a wedge was placed. Frustration arose in many areas. Then frustration turned into anger, because I couldn't control what was going on around me. I couldn't control how donors responded to my appeals, and I couldn't control the feast and famine cycles of my husband's business. I mean, why didn't anyone want an air-conditioner installed in the dead of winter? I was frustrated, and I wanted him to make his phone ring.

Staying in this spiral of frustration and anger only led to bitterness. And I had willingly hopped onto the ride of Thunderation as it spiraled and became a force to be reckoned with. I couldn't fight it as it took hold of me. And it made me sick. I didn't know how to get off the ride.

It wasn't until one day when I was preaching to my daughter about how to handle a situation that I could see much more objectively, because I wasn't the one standing in her shoes. She was frustrated. She couldn't understand why she was often the third wheel, the odd man out. The boys frequently played boy games together or wanted boy time or brother time alone, and she would be standing alone, excluded. She felt rejected. That was something I could identify with.

So I tried to make a distinction between what could be normal sibling rivalry and step-sibling rivalry. It was uncharted water for the both of us. I recalled fighting with my brother almost daily growing up. And there were times I wanted to just play with my Barbies, or with my Strawberry Shortcake dolls, without any interference from him or my three male cousins that lived up the hill.

I had seen enough to know that it was plausible for either of the cases to be true. But regardless of the situation, I had learned that you can't control another person. Period. You can't make someone want to play with you, or even like you. You just have to be who God has called you to be.

As I preached to her, it became very clear to me what was going on. She was frustrated. Then she would let her frustration get the best of her. Every single time. She would lash out, loudly, and say things she shouldn't. And it was easy for me to see, in her case, that her lashing out was not helping at all. It only made things worse. When lashing out didn't produce the result she wanted, her anger festered and turned to bitterness. Over time, I could tell that her negative comments were a symptom of bitterness. I urged her to let it go before it consumed her.

I had been down that road many times before. And what I realized as we drove across a bunch of cotton fields was that she was my "mini-me."

Everything she described — was me. It jumped out at me so clearly. I felt a lump in my throat form, and I fought back tears, because I realized that I had jumped on that crazy train so many times before. That was my pattern: frustration, anger, bitterness. And I was still bitter about several things as I hypocritically preached to her about how to release the need to control someone else.

A dead, stinkin', zombie Pharisee had been resurrected. Just like in *The Walking Dead*. I had stood my ground on so many points, devouring my opponent, and subconsciously believing that the biblical instructions about money did not apply to me.

I had let my high expectations of others elevate my frustrations, and old habits I had once shaken prominently rose to the surface again. I couldn't see what had been going on with me, but I could sure tell you what was going on with someone else. Re-enter scene: dead Pharisee.

I had let my emotions carry me away. I was in a downward spiral of bitterness, and I wanted off the ride. I just didn't know how. Although the realization that I had a crazy cycle of bitterness hit me hard, awareness and acceptance of my tendencies were half the battle. I was still staggering from the bitter revelation when a little more insult was added to the injury. At my own doing, of course. I had another long, unexpected look in the mirror. It happened one day when I was in the attic purging meaningless old junk. Included in the purge was a dusty old trunk that contained mementos dating back to high school. I wondered why I ever felt the need to keep that stuff, because I had never opened the trunk since I'd stuffed the contents in it decades before. In fact, that's why all of the junk had been missed in previous purges. It simply sat there collecting dust.

So when I opened it up and grumbled at the mess before me, I was intrigued by the things I had rat-holed once upon a time. It felt like going through someone else's stuff, and that had me even more curious about this mystery person.

And then it happened. Mystery person had kept a few letters documenting a string of failed relationships over the decades. Why?

I don't know. But there they were. Perhaps God inspired her to unknowingly keep them for this very moment, an invaluable teaching opportunity for future me. Every single one of them expressed a wish to just make me happy.

You cannot imagine how piercing this was for me. Because I knew I was angry. Bitter. I had heard my husband declare this many times before. And every single time he did, I dismissed it. It broke my heart that I wasn't wise enough to just listen to this observation the first time it had been spoken to me. How much heartache and destruction had my years of blindness caused?

The past was dead and gone. It couldn't be changed. And I was happy to leave it there. But my husband was the one unsuspecting victim of my venom that was not part of my past. It frightened me that he might soon become part of my past if I didn't make a change. I had been like General Sherman burning a path of destruction through Georgia during the Civil War; I was about to burn down my own house. I wept. And I knew I couldn't change another soul, but I could change me through the power of Jesus.

My eyes were opened, and the attic became a room of mirrors I never wanted to look in again. One look was enough. It was exponentially worse than those mirrors you encounter during swimsuit season that make you declare you'll never go swimming again. It wasn't a pretty sight.

The winds were changing. God was up to something. I had weathered some rains before, and it had taught me a great deal. And even if God had more stormy gales waiting for me, I still knew He was my umbrella, so I grabbed hold, because somethin' was brewin', something was 'bout to begin.

CHAPTER 17:

TOOLS FOR DISCOVERY & DISCUSSION

1. How do you define security? Has your definition of security ever been tested?

2. How has your view of finances affected your faith?

CHAPTER 17: A SEARCH FOR BIBLICAL TRUTH

THE SOURCE OF SECURITY

Jesus tells us in John 16:33 that we will have trouble in this world, but to have good cheer because He has overcome the world. It's good to be affirmed that God loves us especially when we find ourselves in trouble. Jesus does this for us in John 16:27.

When it comes to dealing with trouble, we can easily glean from David, a beloved servant of God, because he recorded many of his prayers in the book of Psalms. Often David's security was threatened, and he prayed to the Lord, "In You I put my trust." We learn how David intimately poured his heart out to God and trusted Him for deliverance from his fears, daily sorrows, and enemies. When our security is threatened, or perhaps we feel alone, trapped, or abandoned, let the words of David remind us about the character and strength of God, and let our faith rest in Him alone.

What does David write in Psalm 11:4 and Psalm 3:3-4? Who is on the throne? Does He hear our prayers? Why does He bother with all our requests? David wondered the same thing in his distress. Read Psalm 8:3-4. God minds because we are the apple of His eye (Psalm 17:8). As believers, we must remember that Jesus is our hope and our inheritance. He is the prize. Contrast Psalm 17:13-14 and Psalm 16:5-6. Sometimes we may be discouraged by our perceived lack of supply in comparison with our perception of our neighbor's abundance or success, but is our treasure the things of this earth or what is yet to come? In times when our security has been threatened and we lie awake at night in fret, read Psalms 3:5, 4:8, and 17:15. Who sustains? Who gives us safety, security, and satisfaction? As we realign our focus from the troubling things of this world to the throne of grace where every heartfelt petition is received, let us rest in peace and trust Him for safety and provision.

CHAPTER 18

Fed Up

A Slippery Slope

It took a while to process the heaviness of what I had seen in the mirror maze of my attic. And it did feel like a maze, because I wasn't sure how to find the exit or what to do with it exactly. I'm a slow thinker. I have to chew on things for a while and process them before I take action, thus the long delay in accepting the call to the ministry.

All of my pondering made me think of a trip to Colorado back in high school, which led to a profound revelation. This high-school trip was different from the others, because my family let me take my best friend. We had hiked several miles up a steep trail to a beautifully clear mountain lake. It nestled at the bottom of a large basin, and, even though it was summertime, there were still large patches of snow on the rocky peaks above the lake.

My brother, my friend, and I thought it'd be fun to hike up to a seemingly small patch of snow while the rest of the family stayed behind to fish. Once we got to the patch, we realized it wasn't so little. My brother had the bright idea to slide down the narrow but lengthy patch. There was only one problem: the patch of snow ended about a hundred feet below; at the end of the slide were rocky boulders, and on the other side of the boulders was a sheer drop-off. Lacking good sense, we all agreed it would be fun to give it a try. We rarely had snow at home and, when we did, it was on a horizontal plane not conducive to sledding. So we came up with a plan. My friend and I would station ourselves on either side of the narrow patch and catch my brother before he passed the point of no return.

It was like Cousin Eddy in *Christmas Vacation*. He started down the slope, and he was going so stinkin' fast that there could have been flames coming from his rear, but I wouldn't have known, because the instant he flashed past us, snow plowed into my face and stuck to my glasses. I couldn't see anything, and all I could hear was my friend yelling, "Did you catch him?"

My heart sank, because nothing was in my grip, and I had been hoping she caught him. I cleared my glasses, and we looked down the mountain. Thankfully, a big boulder was the one thing strong enough to catch him. It was a serious but funny moment that we laughed about for years. Likewise, I look back and laugh at some serious moments in my life. Once on a slippery slope, it's hard to stop. And often we are blinded and left grasping at the wind. But, thank God, He is the rock that keeps us from going too far.

The Fluctuation of Snares
Destructive patterns had been revealed to me in that necessary look in the mirror to see the cycles I had been repeating. It was the whisper of, "Didn't you catch it?" Was I so blinded that I didn't catch it all the first time around? It's not that I wanted to repeat the cycle

all over again. I just couldn't see the snares that held me captive and how they fed my discontentment.

After all those years, I was finally able to draw lines of distinction to specific snares that I had walked into, beginning with my journey to college, and all throughout my first marriage.

Looking back, it was a progressive outline, easy to chart. Snares that led to my discontentment:

Greed

    Self-Sufficiecy/Control

        Impatience

            Frustration

                Anger

                    Bitterness

                        Hypocrisy/Judgmentalism

                      Unforgiveness

The more I reflected upon my journey, the more I was fascinated by what I saw. After going to Mexico and after my divorce, God began removing these snares one by one, in reverse order, and freeing me from their grip. Why? Because my eyes were so intently fixed upon Him with little distraction during this time. It was easy to point out the things I no longer struggled with.

                    Unforgiveness

                Hypocrisy/Judgmentalism

            Bitterness

        Anger

    Frustration

Impatience

Although I wanted to believe I had been healed of self-sufficiency, greed, and the need to be in control, the truth was that I hadn't been. They still had me blindfolded and tangled as I had repeatedly dismissed any mention of these tendencies. And then I began to see the pattern swell back out, and repeat itself again the moment I remarried. Unintentionally, of course.

Impatience

Frustration

Anger

Bitterness

Hypocrisy/Judgmentalism

Unforgiveness

After having an aha! moment during the pep talk with my daughter, and divinely stumbling into a long, ugly look in the attic mirror, and ultimately charting out the repetitive destructive patterns of my past, I was at a crossroads. Would I allow God to change me before I had another defeat on my journey? Would I find contentment? Would I ever have a laughing place? Yet again, I had a decision to make.

A Powerful Bad Mood

Uncle Remus told another story to little Johnny when the defeated young lad was ready to high-tail it to Atlanta and get as far away as he could from the plantation. Away from all his worries. He had his knapsack loaded and was beginning his journey when Uncle Remus found him on the trail. Immediately, Uncle Remus distracted him by telling him a story of Brer Rabbit being in a "powerful bad mood."

Uncle Remus had a way of painting a picture for Johnny so that the story bore a striking resemblance to his own troubles. And after pondering his stories for a while, young Johnny finally made the connections. So Uncle Remus told him the tale about a time when he found Brer Rabbit packing up to hit the trail, too.

Brer Rabbit: That ol' briar patch ain't brought me nuthin' but trouble and mo' trouble. This is where my trouble is [briar patch, as he boards up his house] and this is the place I belongs away from.

Uncle Remus: Don't you know you can't run away from trouble?

Brer Rabbit: Where I'm goin', there ain't gonna be no trouble.

Uncle Remus: There ain't no place that far.

Brer Rabbit: Well...just the same. I done made up my mind and I ain't never coming back again.

Just like Johnny, and just like Brer Rabbit, I was in a powerful bad mood, and I was fed up. I had just about convinced myself that being alone would get me out of most of my trouble. After all, it's hard to argue with oneself, I reasoned. But I'm thankful that God, like Uncle Remus, intervened and showed me that running away wouldn't cure anything.

If we're honest, there are days when we just want to pack up, like Brer Rabbit, and get as far away from trouble as possible. This is how I'd felt many times before. I had prayed for God's will in so many areas of my life, but there was something still holding me back. Something I couldn't put my finger on.

Spiritual Warfare

God's timing is perfect, and it was His time to begin showing me the significance of spiritual warfare. I had gone through two different studies on Revelation, and God began showing me how much I didn't know about supernatural things, things we can't see here on earth. He showed me so many Scriptures with nuggets of truth that taught me more about the spiritual realm than I had ever known before. It was amazing to me that I had never given it more thought. Of course, I knew that spiritual warfare was real and that the Devil was the great enemy of our souls, but I felt like I had not given proper credit where it was due, not even to the Devil.

Satan is crafty. He is a liar. And his sole mission is to keep one from Christ. For those who already belong to Christ, he is on mission to steal our joy. It discredits our witness as Christian believers if we walk around defeated by the thorns of life. Why would anyone want to become a Christian if we all look miserable? And that is exactly why Satan targets us.

I had to give Satan a few points on the scoreboard for cleverly trapping me, again, and there may have been times where he won the battle, but, rest assured, he won't win the war. We are given that prophecy in Revelation, and that is a truth to deposit in the spiritual bank.

It became very clear to me that I had been severely oppressed by the demons under his command. Nobody wants to talk about this kind of thing, because nobody wants to admit that they're a victim of such oppression. I mean, we want to think we're smarter than that, right? And nobody wants to sound kooky, including me.

But it's real. I wasn't walking around possessed like you'd see in a Hollywood horror film, because the Spirit of Christ dwells within a Christian believer, and how can demons inhabit the same space as the Holy One? They can't. But I was, without question, under attack by the enemy. And I hadn't really looked at it intently from that perspective before.

I was reading about the demon-possessed man living in the tombs when a fresh realization struck me. Another aha! moment. Of course, I knew Jesus had power, but I hadn't given much consideration to the power He has over the enemy, power that I freely have direct access to.

> "Then they sailed to the country of Gadarenes, which is opposite Galilee. And when He stepped out on the land, there met Him a certain man from the city who had demons for a long time. And he wore no clothes, nor did

he live in a house but in the tombs. When he saw Jesus, he cried out, fell down before Him, and with a loud voice said, 'What have I to do with You, Jesus, Son of the Most High God? I beg You, do not torment me!' For He had commanded the unclean spirit to come out of the man. For it had often seized him, and he was kept under guard, bound with chains and shackles; and he broke the bonds and was driven by the demon into the wilderness. Jesus asked him saying, 'What is your name?' And he said, 'Legion,' because many demons had entered him. And they begged Him that He would not command them to go out into the abyss. Now a herd of swine was feeding there on the mountain. So they begged Him that He would permit them to enter them. And He permitted them."
Luke 8:26–32

Everything in Scripture is divinely inspired. So here is what we know about this account in simplest terms:

1. A man was bound by demons for a long time.

2. He lived isolated amongst the dead in the tombs.

3. The oppressive demons knew who Jesus was.

4. They were terrified of Him.

5. Jesus had absolute control over the demons.

6. Jesus healed the man.

There's so much more we could unpack in that passage, but for simplicity's sake, demons are no match for Jesus. They cannot defeat us, cause us to run around crazy, and live as poor, isolated wretches unless we allow them to.

When I read this passage I thought, "That is me." I had been bound by something I hadn't properly identified, taunted so much that I felt emotionally dead, living in a tomb of flesh. In my own strength, I was tossed to and fro by these forces that were much bigger than me. My eyes were opened, and I was tired of chasing a fake rabbit in big circles like a greyhound at the dog track. I was tired of taking the bait, like the dog, and being tempted and ensnared by the same dang things over and over again. It was a vicious cycle, and this dog finally realized how clever the enemy had been in getting her to run down the same old path.

I didn't fully understand it, but since I was being enlightened to their sneaky little games, I was ready to fight back and pack a punch. I knew the One who could absolutely get the demons off my back, to keep me from stumbling and walking straight back into old snares. And I was a woman desperate for healing, just like the one mentioned a few verses later in Luke.

> "Now a woman, having a flow of blood for twelve years, who had spent all her livelihood on physicians and could not be healed by any, came from behind and touched the border of His garment. And immediately her flow of blood stopped. And Jesus said, 'Who touched Me?' When all denied it, Peter and those with him said, 'Master, the multitudes throng and press You, and You say, 'Who touched Me?' But Jesus said, 'Somebody touched Me, for I perceived power going out from Me.' Now when the woman saw that she was not hidden, she came trembling; and falling down before Him, she declared to Him in the presence of all the people the reason she had touched Him and how she was healed immediately. And He said to her, 'Daughter, be of good cheer; your faith has made you well. Go in peace.'" Luke 8:43–48

Again, here is a simple synopsis of what happened:

1. The woman had tried everything, apart from Jesus, to be healed.

2. After 12 years of being sick, she was desperate.

3. She *knew* Jesus could heal her.

4. Nothing would stand in her way of touching His healing garment. Not even a barricade of bystanders.

5. She pushed through, and His power instantly healed her.

6. He knew who had touched Him, but He wanted her to be an example of faith to those who were watching.

I confessed, in prayer, that I was fed up. Exhausted. I cried my eyes out, and told Him I was tired of feeling the way I did. I never fully understood how powerful spiritual warfare could be, and why I had been unable to escape it until then. Like countless times before, I had not been relying on the power of Christ. That was the key.

Classic Philip syndrome, I was trying to operate in my own strength and work with things I could tangibly see. I was trying to figure out how to snatch myself out of the snares of frustration, anger, bitterness, and enemy oppression all on my own. I was trying to figure out what to do with the revelation of my destructive cycles and discontentment, what to do to change myself, how to respond differently in adversity, and, all the while, the chains that bound me to the tombs were tightening so that I was hopelessly surrendered to my own weakness, muttering, "It can't be done."

But thankfully, Jesus gracefully intervened. He allowed me to walk down that path and "showed me" what spiritual warfare looked and felt like in the darkest, deepest sense so that I could truly appreciate the magnificent power that He carries. To "show me" that I can't fight my battles in my own strength. And whether my opponent is seen or unseen, I came to know that I simply need to rely on Him and His power alone. That's all I really needed to do, speak His name, set it at His feet, and leave it there.

I realized I hadn't truly asked Jesus to free me from the bondage of my past, believing that He would. And I hadn't really asked Him to protect me from the demons that were making me miserable. They had learned my patterns. They knew where I was weak, and they knew how to persistently taunt me with the bait that would ultimately rob me of my joy. They did this much longer than I care to admit.

We look at greyhounds and think how dumb they must be to run around in circles every single race. And they do it again, straight out of the gate, every single time it's opened. I was guilty of doing the same thing.

Like the woman who had been sick for so long, I finally knew that Jesus was my only hope and that the enemy simply could not stand in His presence as I proclaimed His power, through prayer, like I'd never done before.

And just as the woman had been instantly healed in the crowd, once I reached for Jesus in absolute faith, I physically felt the burden lifted. The sound of chains bursting and releasing me from my bondage was music to my ears. At the sound of His name, the enemy had no choice but to high-tail it out of Dodge. Tears stained my face as I knew I had instantly been healed. It was a newfound freedom and incomprehensible power like I had never experienced before. Praise Jesus.

CHAPTER 18:

TOOLS FOR DISCOVERY & DISCUSSION

1. Have you ever felt like running away when times got tough? Why is withdrawal and isolation as a coping mechanism unhealthy?

2. Have you considered how significant spiritual warfare might be in your daily life? Can you name a time when you've been under the enemy's oppression?

3. Do you believe the enemy is smart enough to learn your patterns and target you where you are most weak?

CHAPTER 18: A SEARCH FOR BIBLICAL TRUTH

SPIRITUAL BATTLES

We are in a war, a spiritual battle. In order to claim victory we must be prepared. In the passage 2 Corinthians 10:3-6, Paul instructs that we do not war according to what? The weapons we use are mighty in God for pulling down what? A stronghold is anything that hinders an intimate relationship with God. So what do these weapons look like that will help us battle the strongholds in our lives? Read Ephesians 6:10-18. We know the devil will attack so we clothe ourselves with the armor of God and rely on the Spirit for help.

What are some ways the devil will attack? First, he will try to attack our minds and manipulate our thoughts. What does 2 Corinthians 10:5 tells us to hold captive? Our thoughts. Why? Because Satan loves to deceive us with lies (John 8:44), and if he can get us to believe a perversion of God's truth just as he did Eve in the Garden of Eden, then we will fall prey to his wicked schemes (2 Corinthians 11:3).

Next, Satan will try to attack our bodies and health. We know God allowed Satan to attack Job. Read also Mark 9:14-29 and Luke 13:10-17. What kind of spirits bound these people? Who was responsible for these infirmities (Luke 13:16)? What three things can we do to fight back (Mark 9:23, 29)?

Another area Satan tries to attack is our will power. He can torment us through relentless trials hoping we will give up faith and eventually begin to live outside of God's will, but it is God who holds us steady and keeps us in His will (Philippians 2:13). Read 2 Corinthians 4:7-9. We may be frail equipment, but inside these vessels are an unspeakable treasure and power that will never let us be destroyed.

CHAPTER 19

The Power of Prayer

A Thorn is Given

There was no mistaking the source of my newfound freedom. My prayer did pack a punch, and it wasn't from any power of my own. Jesus freed me from the enemy's grip and taught me a valuable lesson.

I became acutely aware of how generic some of my prayers had been. They often lacked details and fervency. It was easy to preach to my daughter against her cookie-cutter prayers, like "Lord, help me have a good day,"—not that there's anything wrong with that prayer. We must bring all things to the throne of grace. Big and little. But my problems stemmed from a lack of faith and not recognizing when God had answered my prayers. Let's face it. We have a 50/50 chance of having a good day. It's either going to be good or bad. So how do we know when God is actively answering our petitions if we aren't being specific?

Further, I realized I had been putting God in a box, as it were, and I wasn't acknowledging Him and the incomprehensible power He has. I would ask for things that were mediocre. Doable. I seldom asked for things that seemed impossible. Perhaps, again, because I lacked the faith to believe He could, and actually would, do the impossible in my life — and being free from past hurts and destructive patterns felt impossible.

So, I began asking for Him to move mountains, with specific detail, so I would know it was a result of His response and His power when the prayer was answered. I also asked for little things, affirmations, and such. And what I began to notice is the timing of His answers, sometimes immediately, and sometimes by the end of the day. As for the prayers that I felt like He wasn't answering, well, I knew He had a purpose for that, too. There was something bigger He was producing within me. And the lack of an answer didn't necessarily mean "no," but perhaps just "not yet."

Then again, I knew that sometimes the answer was, in fact, "no." We can learn this from the apostle Paul, who had been chosen to receive a marvelous glimpse of Heaven, a privilege no one else on earth had been given. God knew there was temptation for Paul to become arrogant and proud as he continued in his ministry sharing the visions he had seen. Again, we see the sovereignty of God at work.

> "For though I might desire to boast, I will not be a fool; for I will speak the truth. But I refrain, lest anyone should think of me above what he sees me to be or hears from me. And lest I should be exalted above measure by the abundance of the revelations, a thorn in the flesh was given to me, a messenger of Satan to buffet me, lest I be exalted above measure. Concerning this thing I pleaded with the Lord three times that it might depart from me. And He

said to me, 'My grace is sufficient for you, for My strength is made perfect in weakness.' Therefore, most gladly I will rather boast in my infirmities, that the power of Christ may rest upon me." 2 Corinthians 12:6–9

Here is what we see in this passage:

1. A thorn was given to Paul.

2. A messenger of Satan was allowed to torment him.

3. Paul begged the Lord three times to take it away.

4. The answer was no.

5. Paul was still protected by God's grace and the power of Christ.

God simply told him "no." How often are we tempted to take credit for major accomplishments in our lives? We may not set out to take full credit, but often, when comments are made, there is temptation to think more of ourselves than we should. Paul could have easily thought, "I'm so special that God chose me above all those other sinners, and because I'm better than them, I was able to get a foretaste of Paradise." God divinely allowed a thorn in Paul's flesh. What was the catalyst God chose to keep Paul humble and reliant on Him? The enemy.

We see other examples in Scripture where God's sovereignty allowed trial for a greater purpose. Such was the case with Job. A conversation took place between God and Satan, and Job would be the object of demonstration. God's purpose for Job's trial was to show Satan that Job was God-fearing, upright, and blameless. He gave Satan permission to put Job through the wringer, because He knew that Job truly loved Him and would not deny Him.

"Then Satan answered the Lord, 'Does Job fear God for nothing? Have You not made a hedge about him and his house and all that he has, on every side? You have blessed the work of his hands, and his possessions have increased in the land. But put forth Your hand now and touch all that he has; he will surely curse You to Your face.' Then the Lord said to Satan, 'Behold, all that he has is in your power, only do not put forth your hand on him.' So Satan departed from the presence of the Lord." Job 1:9–12

First, Satan acknowledged that God had a hedge of protection around His servant Job. Second, Satan's prediction about Job's faithfulness without the hedge was wrong.

As we read through the book of Job, we learn that the man's life was miserable as Satan was allowed to take all that he had: material possessions, children, health. Even those who remained unscathed, his wife and friends, turned against Job and insisted that the calamity must have been the result of his sin. They had no knowledge of the conversation between God and Satan, no knowledge of the true purpose behind the test.

Satan ended up eating a nasty piece of humble pie, because Job did love God, and not just because of all the riches he had been given.

Heightened awareness of spiritual warfare taught me to accept the fact that sometimes the enemy is allowed to knock us around a bit for a higher refining purpose, for God's glory. Some may struggle with that concept, but I realized that our Advocate is not sitting idly on the sidelines. He has actively fought my battles, and there is no question in my mind who is supremely in charge. I've learned to follow His command, even if it is on the front lines in enemy territory.

Jesus loves us. Wildly. With unparalleled passion. We have sixty-six books of canonized Scripture to prove it. And I love the little nuggets we can pull from Luke chapter 22.

"And the Lord said, 'Simon, Simon! Indeed, Satan has asked for you, that he may sift you as wheat. But I have prayed for you, that your faith should not fail; and when

you have returned to Me, strengthen your brethren.'"
Luke 22:31–32

Again, Satan was asking for a servant of the Lord. We aren't told what the specific response was, but we are told that Jesus prayed for Peter. He prays for me. And He prays for you. He is our high priest, and the only One in whom we can find access to the Father and eternal life. He's not sitting by with His hands folded, wondering what will happen while all of hell is trying to take as many souls as it can. He is actively petitioning for me and for you.

There is a war, and while the supernatural forces surge around us, most of us never even recognize what can't been seen with the naked eye.

Satan asked for Job. He asked for Simon Peter. And don't think for one single second that the enemy hasn't asked for you, too.

But don't be afraid, because earlier in Luke we are told who trumps whom when it comes to authority and power. Jesus was instructing His seventy disciples:

> "Then the seventy returned with joy, saying, 'Lord, even the demons are subject to us in Your name.' And He said to them, 'I saw Satan fall like lightning from heaven. Behold, I give you the authority to trample on serpents and scorpions, and over all the power of the enemy, and nothing shall by any means hurt you.'" Luke 10:17–19

Where did their power come from? Jesus. He freely gave them authority and power. They didn't have magical powers on their own, and neither do we. The all-powerful Creator was, and is, and always will be, the true source of power.

So how do we get power from Him? We simply ask for it.

Fighting on Our Knees
My prayer life needed an overhaul, and I am thankful the scales were removed from my eyes so I could see more clearly how impotent

I had been against the powers of hell. I hadn't been praying and believing in the power of the Spirit.

So what changed?

My prayers became more intimate and more meaningful. I finally had some faith to stand behind what it was I asked for.

I believed in the truth and promise in Scripture.

I believed my prayers would be heard.

I believed my requests aligning with His will would be answered.

With each spiritual marker on my journey, I have learned more about God. This fact will remain as long as I walk the face of this earth. He is infinitely more than I can comprehend or imagine. And as each spiritual milestone passes, I will learn even more about how much He loves me and how much He is worthy of my trust.

My prayers are no longer being sent up to a disconnected being in the sky about whom I know very little. There's a difference in head knowledge and heart knowledge. I now know, with all my heart, I am approaching Almighty God, Abba, Father, when I pray.

My husband has a name. I love how it rolls off my tongue. How it bounces around in my head. How it resonates in my heart. So, it wouldn't be as intimate if I went around calling him by his title, Husband, or addressing him as "mechanical genius," although he might appreciate the sentiment the first few times I tried it. He has a personal name, and I love to use it.

So, why wouldn't we want to use God's personal name? Doesn't it affectionately warm His heart just as it would our spouse? After all, isn't the Christian faith all about having a relationship with Him?

When I prayed, I began using the Old Testament Hebrew personal names of God that I had learned in another divinely timed study. If I was struggling with fear over finance, I called upon Jehovah-Jireh, the God who provides. If I was feeling alone, I talked to El Roi, the God who sees. If I felt like I needed to be healed, I petitioned Jehovah-Rapha, the God who heals. And so on. Each name describes an attribute of the one true living God, Yahweh, and each account is recorded in Scripture describing the circumstances in which the name originated.

After making these changes and documenting how my prayers were being answered, I was more fearless than ever before.

One of the most transforming books I've read aside from Scripture itself is *Fervent*, by Priscilla Shirer. In this book, the author does an excellent job of pointing out the strategies of the enemy, and she brings a fresh awareness to the craftiness behind the enemy of our souls. One quote from her book has stuck with me. She declares, "Prayer is the portal that brings the power of heaven down to earth," and, boy, is that ever true!

I began plastering verses, quotes, and sayings all over the corner where I began faithfully getting on my knees and talking to Jesus. I was untouchable, crouched there with my face to the ground, and I knew the words of missionary Corrie ten Boom were spot-on when she said, "Don't pray when you feel like it. Have an appointment with the Lord and keep it. A man is powerful on his knees." Amen, sister.

There were days I didn't feel like praying. When I'd rather be lazy and sit watching TV. Or make excuses in the midst of chaos about not having a quiet space to go and take care of business. But business, indeed, I had.

There were still days when God allowed those thorns to poke and prod me, but I had learned that lashing back and trying to take matters into my own hands was fruitless. And this was when I taped Hudson Taylor's advice to my wall. "It is possible to move men, through God, by prayer alone."

Since the massive transformation in my prayer life, I resolved to fight my battles on my knees. And whenever any nemesis is kept at bay and I am protected, I will know beyond a shadow of a doubt, and based on the evidence shown, that my specific petitions are being answered only by the hand of the Lord and not from any finagling of my own. There is absolute power in prayer.

Did Someone Ask for Me, Again?

When we discover the gems on our spiritual journey, does it mean that we won't ever be tested again? Of course not. Paul continued having a thorn. And so did I. But the snares of bitterness that had so often brought me down due to circumstantial events no longer had a hold on me. Nor did the need to control, or to rely on a steady paycheck. They no longer dominated my thoughts and actions. The desire to fall on my knees prevailed instead.

Our family wasn't immune to grief, either. It still came our way. And the more we tried to live for Jesus, the more it felt like the enemy had us in his crosshairs, most likely hoping we'd give up. He's an opportunist, and any of us committed to faith make alluring targets.

Opportunity struck when my husband and I found out we would be parents again. For me, more than a decade had passed, and I had longed for another child, deeply. In that time, I found great empathy for barren women who also longed to have children. For whatever reason, it seemed that having another child was not part of God's plan for me. But then it happened! We were delightfully surprised, and although I was cautiously hesitant to announce the news so early because of my inherently high-risk status, my husband just couldn't contain himself. He shouted it from the rooftops, and I gladly joined in on the blissful fun of making our announcement.

We were elated, until a week later, when obvious signs of complications appeared. We went to the doctor and had tests performed only to confirm our worst fears. I wept.

At the earliest sign of complication, I had sent word to my prayer warriors. They continued to pray for us. For weeks I wondered why I didn't cry much after our loss, but I know without a doubt that the prayers of friends and loved ones carried me through and sustained my strength. God showed incredible favor and gave amazing peace that swaddled me through the entire situation.

When weeks had begun to pass, I began to feel like Smaug the dragon from *The Hobbit*, but only in the sense of having impenetrable armor. I was pleased that I wasn't wallowing in grief. However, any *Hobbit* fan knows the one flaw in Smaug's armor. There was a chink in his breastplate that eventually allowed an arrow to penetrate and bring him down.

This is where the enemy entered the scene, striking while the iron was hot. Something was said to me one day, and just as that iron arrow took down Smaug the dragon at his weakest spot, so did those words. So much for being ten-feet tall and bulletproof! It was all I could do to stay composed until I had scrambled into the quiet darkness of our closet at home, where I could fall on my knees and just come unglued. It was there that I accepted the invitation to the pity party, party of two. My invisible, but oh-so-real, lying companion played on my insecurities in the darkness as he whispered accusations in my ear. "This is why you can't have any more children. This is why you lost the baby. This is why you're an unfit mother."

Trust me, once he dug his claws into me, I physically felt dragged into a pit of despair. I don't really know how long it lasted, but I am proud to announce that was the only pity party I had for the unfortunate event.

I may have been an unsuspecting victim at a not-so-fun party, but the hero of this story is my precious Jesus, because as I lay in my dungeon of despair, sobbing, beaten down, not even knowing what to pray, the one thing I do recall praying was that I just needed to feel His presence. I just needed the pain to dissolve, and in that very moment, in the quietness of my dark closet, yet another prayer was answered.

I could hear the kids, who were oblivious to my meltdown, upstairs rambling around doing their thing. And then I heard it: the Hallelujah Chorus from Handel's Messiah. My daughter, who loves to sing, often belts out a tune from a random genre. It could be Country. It could be Pop. It could even be a commercial jingle. It doesn't matter. She has a large repertoire to choose from, and there's no telling what may come out of her mouth, or when or where. Even in a public bathroom. But in my dark moment, she started singing the Hallelujah Chorus, and I know for certain it was not by chance.

If you don't believe in spiritual warfare, I'm telling you it is real. I've got claw marks on my heels to prove it, and that's just one of many times. So why is the enemy so persistent in trying to bring me down? Because he knows I have a big mouth. He knows I'm going to write about it. Talk about it. Tell my story. And perhaps he hopes that one of his attempts will cause me to lose faith. And shut my mouth. That's my best guess. I don't always know why bad things happen to people. I don't know why we lost our baby. I just know Who carried me through the storm.

"What exactly are the lyrics of Handel's Messiah?" Among all the repeated hallelujahs are these words: "For the Lord God omnipotent reigneth... and He shall reign forever and ever. King of kings, and Lord of lords, forever and ever." I had prayed to feel His presence, and these words were a beautiful reminder of Who is on the throne. And who is not. I did feel His bold presence, and in that moment I was snatched from the talons of the evil one. Just like that. In addition to feeling His presence, I was reminded of the precious being He has already gifted me with and allowed me to birth, the beautiful creature upstairs singing the Hallelujah Chorus. She truly has no clue what a gift she is. He gave her to me. And that was no mistake.

And finally, even if it only lasted for a brief time, I was reminded of the immense joy we experienced that week over a child we will never meet this side of eternity. But one day we will. Being a parent is one of the most indescribable blessings one will ever experience. For that I am thankful.

Finding My Laughing Place

A little time had passed, and one night I couldn't sleep. I was troubled. I rolled out of bed while everyone else slept and went to the kitchen table. It was completely dark. I sat down and wept over the thing that was troubling me.

I prayed to the One who never rests, and I confessed my struggle and told Him, "This must be one of those thorns You've chosen not to remove." And just as I whispered those words, His instantaneous response silenced me. His response illuminated my mind with precise clarity. It was the closest I've ever experienced to an audible response from Him. His words were confidently unmistakable as He said, "But My blood covered every one of those thorns."

Every... one... of those thorns.

Salty streams dripped onto the table where I sat, and I was left speechless. I giggled a little and thought, "Well, that settles it." What rebuttal did I have to that? So that's where I left it and went back to sleep, peacefully. Laughter through tears, such a refreshingly rare combination that is somehow so freeing.

He was right. Powerfully right. The crown of thorns He wore on the cross, and the blood He shed was for me, and for you. Nothing escapes His sight, and we are eternally safe inside the loving grip of His hands. His grace is sufficient. And His power is perfect in my weakness. Therefore, my weakness is an asset. And with that, I am completely content.

There was a time I was dying to find my laughing place. But not anymore. Finding it has been quite a journey. It took chasing a number of dead ends for me to realize that only the power of Jesus is going to give me the peace and contentment I've always yearned for. Nothing else on this earth will give lasting satisfaction.

Discovering the power of prayer has been key to unlocking the fullness of joy with my relationship with Christ. He is my laughing place. My laughing partner. Because anything this old life throws at me is no match for Him. He has proven it to me time and time again.

I reflect back on tales from my childhood. Brer Rabbit knew where his laughing place was. And now, so do I.

I laugh at the resilience of Brer Rabbit, and how he never let the enemy make him feel defeated. Even when he was tied up on a skewer and, by all appearances, had very little hope left, he knew how to get out of trouble. For him, it was his quick wit that always prevailed against his foes. That was his superpower. We have to know how to get out of trouble, too. To not lose hope. To know where our superpower comes from. It's from Jesus.

Uncle Remus told Johnny many tales to take his mind off of his worries. I still can't help but smile at these silly folk tales that are over a hundred years old. One of the most popular tales is one of Brer Rabbit and the Tar Baby. Brer Rabbit had been captured yet again by Brer Bear and Brer Fox. In order to get out of that particular bind, he begged them not to throw him into the briar patch. Believing it to be a good idea, they threw him into the briar patch, despite his dramatic begging, and they waited for the blood-curdling sounds of death. They waited, and then much to their surprise, they heard laughter! Brer Rabbit had outsmarted them again. He shouted out from beneath a blanket of thorns, "I was bred and born in the briar patch, Brer Fox." And he laughed as he made another clever escape.

We are born in a briar patch, too. Thorns surround us. Perhaps the Lord will remove them. Perhaps He won't. But we must learn to live amongst them and learn to laugh away the sly fox's attempts to bring us down. That is the goal: to be so intimately grounded in our faith with Jesus Christ that we can literally laugh in the face of the enemy, as we know with every fiber of our being that Satan is no match for the power of Christ.

Instead of desperately dying to find temporal solutions to our problems, we must die to ourselves and the attempts to fight our own battles. As Christians, we must abide in the love and power of Jesus. And that is the key to contentment.

CHAPTER 19:

TOOLS FOR DISCOVERY & DISCUSSION

1. Do you only pray mediocre, doable prayers? Have you ever prayed for the impossible and believed God would answer you? Do these prayers align with His will?

2. How do you feel about God using the enemy as the catalyst for a higher refining purpose, His glory?

3. Do you set an appointment for prayer and keep it even when you don't feel like it?

4. Have you prayed in specific detail, telling no one, and waited to see how and when God answers your prayer?

5. Do you recognize that Jesus' blood covered every thorn that troubles you? Do you believe He sees you in your pain? Do you believe He holds you up, gives you power, and protects you against the evil one?

6. Do you see your weaknesses as an asset so that the power of Christ can work in its place? Do you know that God loves and cares for you?

CHAPTER 19: A SEARCH FOR BIBLICAL TRUTH

THE LOVE OF GOD

Perhaps your journey, like mine and so many others, is marked with some trials and suffering. The unspoken question that loomed in my mind and in the depths of my heart during my suffering was, "Does God care?" The apostle Paul suffered much for his decision to follow Christ, but God used him mightily to proclaim the good news of Christ, and he went on to write much of the New Testament. His suffering wasn't in vain, nor is yours. God has a purpose for all things, and they ultimately lead to His glory. Never lose sight of the forest for the trees. God does care, and God does love you.

Paul asks some rhetorical questions in Romans 8:31-39. First, he asks in verse 31, "If God is for us, who can be against us?" Obviously the answer is no one. No one can overpower God. Second, he asks in verse 35, "Who shall separate us from the love of Christ?" Again, the answer is no one. Christ is the ultimate prize, hope, and promise given to the Christian believer. He's God's ultimate display of love (verse 39). Finally, read verse 37. What does Scripture say that we are in all of our sufferings? More than conquerors. Through whom? Jesus. Why? Because He first loved us (1 John 4:19).

EPILOGUE

Leaving a Legacy

Dying to Find My Laughing Place is my story. It's one of redemption and hope. A life forever changed. There's someone out there hungry for truth and longing for hope of their own as they face enormous battles. And if my story is told to thousands of people only to reach one lost, hopeless soul, then I rejoice in living my life as an open book. Trials included. It truly would be an answered prayer.

As mentioned in the Introduction, I dug my heels in and didn't want to write this book. I didn't care to air my dirty laundry for the world to see. To paint a picture of myself that was less than desirable. And after about five years of ignoring people telling me to write a book, it was finally the Lord's voice I couldn't ignore.

Hindsight is 20/20, and as I reflected on my story I had to document the revelation that biblical illiteracy and prayerlessness played dominant roles in my failures. The two bred hopelessness. And, ultimately, I burned out.

But my story didn't stop there. God didn't allow me to wallow in burnout, and He showed me that sometimes we have to walk a mile in someone else's shoes in order to relate to what they're going through. Why is that so important? Because God uses people. He doesn't have to, but often He chooses to use us to reach out to others and help them on their journey.

During this time of reflection, I asked the Lord to give me a vision for my long-term ministry. I didn't realize what I was asking, because in my heart I really thought I'd get a glimpse of what I'd be doing for the next five years at the orphan care ministry where I served.

He began to show me something much different. He began to repeatedly address the issue of burnout, and the pressing need for a quiet place to go pray and spend time alone with Him. In fact, it grabbed my attention so strongly that I went through all the Gospels to jot down every reference I could find of Jesus getting away from the crowds to find a "quiet place" where He could speak to the Father. After all, Jesus is our model. And I knew if He felt it was important, then it must be important for me too.

A glimpse of the vision He had begun to show me regarding a quiet place excited me and had me chasing rabbit trails for almost a year, trying to figure out differing avenues of what it meant. I finally realized that I wouldn't get the rest of the vision until I was obedient in the first thing He asked me to do. And that was write this book. Ugh.

So I packed up and went to my little quiet place, a simple cabin in the mountains, and literally worked from sunup to sundown for two solid weeks on my story. I prayed through the entire project. And after I had a draft and on the last night of my trip, I asked the Lord for the rest of the vision. After all, I reasoned that I was trying to be obedient and finally had a tangible draft of the book in hand.

It was as if He unlocked my mind and flooded the entire night with visions of the most fantastic things He wanted me to do, and it started with creating a new ministry. There were many dimensions and facets to what He showed me, and I have no idea how He will get the new ministry there. But I know He will.

I know that one of my spiritual gifts is compassion. Another is teaching. God doesn't waste talent. Or pain. He has given me a story to which many can relate. And my passion is to reach women with the gospel of Christ and empower them with tools to combat biblical illiteracy and prayerlessness, to get them through their storms and out of the grip of burnout. To not just hobble through the trial, but to burst forth in freedom by tapping into the power that He longs to give us.

One might ask, "Well isn't that the purpose of the church?" Well, yes. It is the purpose of the church. We are the church. Church doesn't have to take place within the four walls of the physical building many attend on Sunday mornings; rather, it is through God's people and the relationships we form as sisters in Christ.

I understand burnout. Being tired. Not just the "I didn't get a good night's sleep" kind of tired but the prolonged struggle kind of tired. I understand not being able to give another ounce of yourself to another being. To be so deflated that you dread getting up in the morning and facing another day. Where the simplest of tasks, like brushing your teeth, can feel like having to conquer the world.

I also understand the power of Christ and how I was snatched up from my pit of despair through Him alone. I want others to taste that victory. I want to encourage them that it's okay to not feel okay. Because I've been there, too. Half the battle of victory sometimes begins with admitting that we aren't "okay." And that's when we allow ourselves to be vulnerable and ask for help. To let go and let the power of Christ heal us.

I know that I can't solve anyone else's problems. Heck, I couldn't even solve my own. I still have issues. But I can introduce you to the One who can solve them. Who can give peace and contentment regardless of the situation. And that means giving someone the tools to work with and the opportunity to do battle.

As I was driving home from my quiet place in the mountains, a vacant historic building caught my eye. Its fantastic façade was nothing more than the dilapidated shell of a former electric power plant. I desperately wanted to find the funds to purchase it in order to house the new ministry, but as I researched further, I learned the building was no longer for sale.

Although I wouldn't be the one renovating the old jewel, the short tangent I followed with the building had significance, as it provided the name for the new ministry springing forth, The Power Plant. How appropriate. It completely encapsulates the vision I've been given.

The Power Plant ministry is for women who are struggling, burned out. It is designed to teach them how to tap into the divine power they've been given through prayer and reading Scripture. I know that the world is a distracting place, so the premise behind the quiet place and how it related to the earliest vision given to me became quite clear. Simply put, retreating to a quiet place with the Lord is key. There we will find renewal and healing.

As women, we are needed. Not that men aren't. This certainly isn't a comparison. God has divine roles for the gents too. I'm just saying that our particular roles are demanding. We serve our husbands. We serve our kids. We often work outside the home in addition to working inside the home. We volunteer for committees. It goes on and on. As for me, I felt it was extremely difficult to find that one place where I wasn't needed. In demand. So that I could take care of urgent business with God without interruption. Having that time became sacred to me. And now, the idea of having a place for other women to enjoy is equally as important.

The Power Plant will provide serene quiet places so women can privately get on their knees to do business with God. Call them prayer pods, prayer cabins, master tree houses, whatever. We shall see how He provides and what it ends up looking like. These prayer cabins will surround a larger lodge that will be a central meeting place where we will bless the socks off women in practical ways like serving a meal, providing light-hearted fun, keeping their kids or special-needs dependents, and teaching them nuggets of truth.

The Power Plant will offer a program that isn't burdensome. Not only will The Power Plant provide outlets to have desperately needed quality time with the Lord —a luxury ladies may not have at home — but we will also provide tools to learn how to find laughter in the midst of their storms.

Brer Rabbit tales were woven into my story and inspired me to find my laughing place, so one of the program elements is designed to pinpoint laughter even when everything is still in chaos. There just isn't enough laughter happening at the bottom of the burnout barrel, and The Power Plant is going to change that!

This is my mission. My legacy. God has allowed me to experience divorce, raising a special-needs child, single parenting, having a blended family, and losing a child. To experience wealth, and to be broke. To feel the depths of darkness and to see the power of light. He's saved me from myself and a whole host of other things for the sole purpose of looking someone in the eye, perhaps another woman at the end of her rope, and saying, "I understand."

It's my calling to help in this area.

Interestingly enough, God is going to use my old desires to build and design for a higher purpose. To not just take for myself, but to give back. This time it'll be for His kingdom's sake.

The Power Plant model is simple. It's one that can be replicated in any location. And I long to see women on their knees across the world, taking back their lives through the power of Christ.

It was my prayer from the inception of this project, and a safeguard to combat any temptation on my part to step into an old snare of greed, to wholly dedicate this book to the Lord. Whatever He decides to do with this story in terms of financial gain, one hundred percent of the net profits will be poured into The Power Plant. This is my promise.

I prayed for vision and God answered. Financing such a grand venture may be intimidating, but Jehovah-Jireh will provide. He always has. And He always will. And that, my friends, will be the ultimate testament of His glory and provision, when Power Plants spring up across the countryside and I can't take an ounce of credit for it!

If you are interested in learning more about The Power Plant, please visit www.thepowerplantms.org. We are on a mission, planting seeds of hope and being grounded in the power of Christ.

To God be the glory.

Bibliography

Lewis, C.S. *The Screwtape Letters.* New York: Macmillan Co., 1943. Print.

MercyMe. Lyrics to "Bring the Rain." Genius, 2017, genius.com/Mercyme-bring-the-rain-lyrics.

Pink, Arthur W. *A Fourfold Salvation.* Bottom of the Hill Publishing, 2011. Print.

Song of the South. Dir. Wilfred Jackson. Perf. James Baskett, Bobby Driscoll, Luana Patten, Ruth Warrick, Lucile Watson, Hattie McDaniel. RKO Radio Pictures, 1946. Film.

Strong, James. *Strong's Exhaustive Concordance of the Bible.* Peabody: Hendrickson Publishers, Inc., 2007. Print.

Vine, W. E. Merrill F. Unger, William White, and W E. Vine. *Vine's Complete Expository Dictionary of Old and New Testament Words.* Nashville: Nelson, 1996. Print.

93027452R00169

Made in the USA
Columbia, SC
08 April 2018